WILLIAMSON

Little Hands

the Little Hands Art Book

Little Hands® and Kids Can!® are registered
trademarks of Williamson Publishing Co.

Library of Congress
Cataloging-in-Publication Data

Press, Judy 1944-
    The little hands art book: exploring arts & crafts
with 2- to 6-year-olds / Judy Press
    p.   cm.
    "A Williamson little hands book."
    Includes index.
    ISBN 0-913589-86-1:
    1. Handicraft—Juvenile literature. (1.Handicraft.)
I.Title.
TT160.P78 1994   94-13910
702'.8—dc20   CIP
                                              AC

Cover design and illustration: Trezzo-Braren Studio
Interior design: Trezzo-Braren Studio
Illustrations: Loretta Trezzo
Printing: Capital City Press

Williamson Publishing Co.
Box 185
Charlotte, Vermont 05445
1-800-234-8791

Manufactured in Mexico

        13 14 15 16 17 18 19 20

Notice: The information contained in this book is
true, complete, and accurate to the best of our
knowledge. All recommendations and suggestions
are made without any guarantees on the part of
the author or Williamson Publishing. The author and
publisher disclaim all liability incurred in connection
with the use of this information.

Dedication

To my four free spirits, Brian, Debbie, Darren, and Matt,
            and
to my husband, Allan, who made everything possible.

A WILLIAMSON LITTLE HANDS BOOK

the Little Hands Art Book

BY JUDY PRESS

illustrated by Loretta Trezzo Braren

WILLIAMSON PUBLISHING • CHARLOTTE, VERMONT 05445

Contents

Markers

Crayons

Recycled & Found Art

Appendix A: Recipes for Homemade Art Supplies

Appendix B: Recycled & Found Art Materials ·

Index ·

Acknowledgements

I am fortunate to have taught art at a number of fine institutions in the greater Pittsburgh area. These classes enabled me to work with very young children and their caregivers. In most instances this was the first time these children participated in an art class. Children came to class with moms and dads, grandmothers and grandfathers, baby-sitters and nannies, siblings and friends, to experience creating together.

I would like to thank the Pittsburgh Center for the Arts, Sweetwater Art Center, Community College of Allegheny County, the Jewish Community Center — South Hills Branch, and the Higher Horizons Program at Baker Elementary School, for their contribution to the arts in their communities and for the opportunity they afforded me to teach the joy of creating to so many young children. I would also like to thank the Children's Department of the Mt. Lebanon Public Library, the Children's Book Writing Group of Mt. Lebanon, Vincent Maccioli, and my family, neighbors, and friends for their support and encouragement.

A Word to Grown-Ups

I began this children's art book by writing poems. It may seem like an unusual way to proceed, but poetry reflects experiences, ideas, and emotions, and is a wonderful way to inspire artistic creation. Each poem in this book reflects the potential inherent in the medium and provides a bridge to the activity itself.

Art is an expression of creativity; it is a process that enhances development and learning in young children. It's an experience that begins with a child's early exploration and manipulation of ideas and materials. It proceeds to a stage of production, during which the creator uses whatever technical skills are required to carry out the project. It is a connection between the inner world of imagination and intuition, and the physical world that surrounds us. Artistic creation reflects who and where we are in the various stages of our growth and development.

Art projects should be open-ended with instructions and demonstrations intended only to suggest possible ways of proceeding. Originality must influence the outcome. Don't allow specific rules and directions to impose on children's imagination and spontaneity. Avoid holding up finished projects as prototypes, as that simply sets limitations on the child's creative response to the poem, the medium, and self-expression.

This is an art book geared toward children between the ages of two and six. Older children may take the projects further and will not need the level of assistance or supervision of the younger child. The projects have been chosen to enhance such skills as eye-hand coordination, small muscle development, problem solving, and decision making. Read the poems at the beginning of the activity, then present the art materials. It may be necessary to demonstrate the technique of working with specific materials, but as the children gain confidence, they will be able to proceed on their own. Use the instructions as general guidelines, allowing for freedom of exploration. Don't be surprised at the amount of time spent squeezing glue — it's all part of learning about the medium.

A Whole Learning Experience

One of the joys of working with children is that they bring all of themselves — their curiosity, their personalities, their fears, their excitement — to bear on every experience. Art is not separate from playing outdoors, or numbers, or imagination, or language. Children are constantly exploring with all of their senses, making wonderful connections that help make sense of the world around them.

Because this openness to the totality of experience is in full bloom in the early years, I have suggested with most of the art in this book ways to extend the experience using other sensibilities. In some cases, a relevant story might be suggested; in others, a walk outdoors to experience the heat of the sun or the coldness of the snow; in yet others, a walk down a street looking for shapes that increase the powers of observation and environmental awareness.

Is this part of art? Very definitely so! The creative experience must always — even from the littlest hands — be an expression of how that small person sees himself or herself in relation to his or her world at that particular moment.

Practical Matters

The materials needed to complete the projects in this book are readily available, and the instructions are direct and easy to follow. Recipes for materials such as play dough and finger paint can be found in Appendix A, and a list of items worth collecting for an "Art Box" at home is in Appendix B. Children should participate in collecting art supplies, in taking care of them, and in clean-up after each use.

Have the following supplies on hand before you begin: safety scissors, white craft glue, tape, package of assorted colors of construction paper, thin white paper, newspaper, shirt cardboard, poster paints in primary colors, tray of watercolor paints, a paintbrush, markers, and crayons (not the fat kind that children find difficult to grasp). Work on newspaper and keep a sponge handy to wipe up the inevitable spills.

Potential art projects can be created from many of the things we discard, so be an industrious scavenger. Keep a sharp eye out for paper products and packaging materials that would end up in landfills. Introduce recycled materials and nature's own bountiful supplies along with store-bought art supplies and watch children's imaginations transform them into unique creations!

Safety First

As a general rule of safety, always do art in a well-ventilated room, assess your young artist's propensity to put small objects in his or her mouth (make appropriate materials decisions accordingly), and work with nontoxic materials. Keep in mind that younger siblings may pick up odds and ends from the floor or pull items off the table's edge.

Most items used in these projects can be handled safely by little hands. Where scissors are used, *please use child safety scissors — never adult sharp scissors.* It is worth investing in a pair of good child safety scissors that can really cut. Cutting is a skill that children develop slowly, so allow them to practice their cutting skills on scraps of paper and be ready to help if your child is not ready to cut with scissors yet.

There is an asterisk (*) in the project's materials list to indicate an item meant for grown-up use only. Where a knife is indicated, please be sure to use a *small, dull butter knife.* Assess your child's readiness when using tools such as staplers and hole punches, too. To prevent any accidents or injuries, very young children should not work directly with these tools. When helping young children, always ask, "Where would you like me to cut?" so the young artist maintains creative control of his or her own project.

When using recycled styrofoam trays, only use those that contained fruits and vegetables. Meat trays — even after washing — may still contain traces of contaminants from uncooked meat. If fruit and vegetable styrofoam trays aren't available to recycle, use a pie tin or piece of cardboard.

Art Is Fun!

It's important to maintain a relaxed atmosphere, where a good time can be had by all who participate in art. If it is a day when spills and self-expression will be too much to handle, then read a story together, instead, and share a hands-on art experience at a more appropriate time. *The Little Hands Art Book* is written for children and the grown-ups in their lives. It provides a wonderful opportunity to spend time together and share in the joy of creating.

Let the Art Start!

This is a book that tells about art,
And gives you ideas to use at the start.
Try doing the projects in your own way,
What you create will be okay.

Put on a smock, an old shirt will do,
Cover the table in newspaper, too.
Art's about feelings that belong to you,
It's a way to discover something brand new!

Before you get started keep this in mind,
Art supplies are easy to find.
There's paint, markers, crayons, glue, and some clay,
These are the things you'll use every day.

Sometimes scissors are hard to understand,
Practice a lot or tear paper by hand.
And you don't have to rush out to the store,
Look around the house and you'll find much more.

There are odd socks, scraps of fabric, and thread,
Try using magazines that have already been read.
There are buttons and paper towel rolls, too,
Spaghetti, brown bags, and even bamboo.

Spills sometimes happen to everyone,
A kitchen sponge gets the clean-up done.
Finger paint is messy, glue is sticky,
But washing your hands isn't too tricky.

Now that you are ready, pull up your seat,
And begin to create something that's neat.
Don't forget to pick up when the work's done,
And get ready for another day of art fun!

GLUE

Glue is very sticky,
and lots of fun to squeeze,
A little dab holds things down,
in case you have to sneeze!

Paper Bag Picnic Baskets

*If breezes blow picnic plates
high into the air,
Use glue to hold them down
until the ants get there!*

HERE'S WHAT YOU NEED

White craft glue

Paper plate

Markers

Child safety scissors

Large brown paper bag

Old magazines

HERE'S WHAT YOU DO

1 Use scissors to cut off top half of the paper bag. Fold over rim of the bag. Cut a handle from the top half; then glue it onto sides of the rim to make a basket.

2 Decorate the basket with markers.

3 Use the scissors to cut pictures of food from old magazines. Glue magazine food pictures onto the paper plate. Place plate in the basket for a picnic.

CUT STRIP FOR HANDLE

CUT BAG BOTTOM FOR BASKET

GLUE HANDLE TO INSIDE OF BASKET

FOLD OVER RIM

GLUE FOOD PICTURES ONTO PAPER PLATES

MORE ART FUN!

☆ Use scissors to cut fringes around the edges of a large sheet of paper. Color paper with markers for a picnic blanket (don't forget to draw the ants!)

☆ Use scissors to cut flowers, bugs, or designs out of construction paper. Glue onto sides of basket.

☆ Talk about your favorite foods to pack in a picnic basket. Describe how they taste: **sweet, salty, sour, spicy.**

Muffin Cup Bird

*Clouds are soft and puffy,
they seem to hang up in the sky,
Bluebirds flap their feathered wings
as they go flying by!*

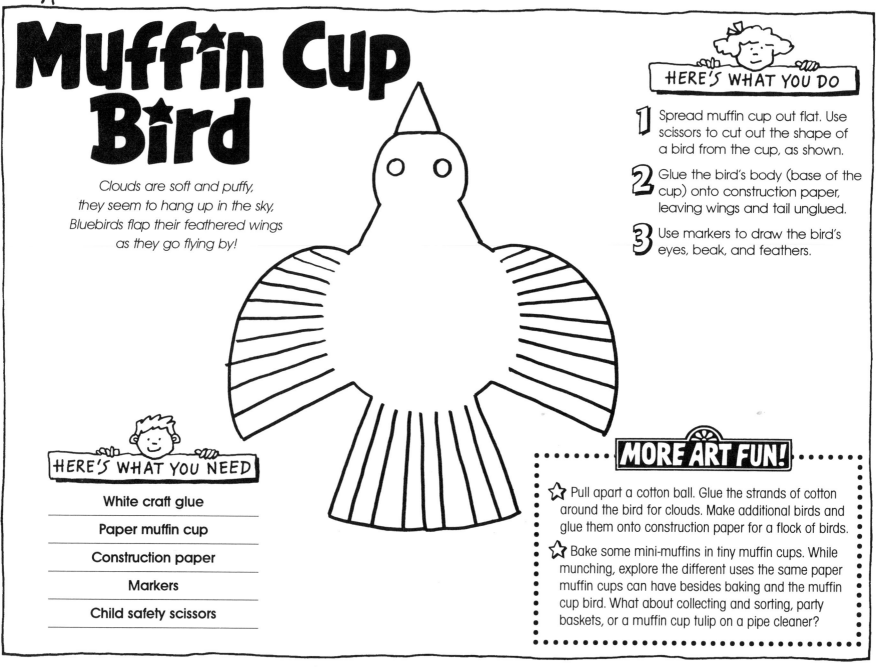

HERE'S WHAT YOU DO

1 Spread muffin cup out flat. Use scissors to cut out the shape of a bird from the cup, as shown.

2 Glue the bird's body (base of the cup) onto construction paper, leaving wings and tail unglued.

3 Use markers to draw the bird's eyes, beak, and feathers.

HERE'S WHAT YOU NEED

White craft glue

Paper muffin cup

Construction paper

Markers

Child safety scissors

MORE ART FUN!

☆ Pull apart a cotton ball. Glue the strands of cotton around the bird for clouds. Make additional birds and glue them onto construction paper for a flock of birds.

☆ Bake some mini-muffins in tiny muffin cups. While munching, explore the different uses the same paper muffin cups can have besides baking and the muffin cup bird. What about collecting and sorting, party baskets, or a muffin cup tulip on a pipe cleaner?

Eggs in a Nest

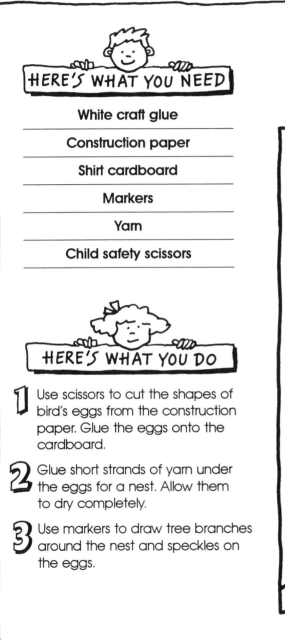

HERE'S WHAT YOU NEED

White craft glue

Construction paper

Shirt cardboard

Markers

Yarn

Child safety scissors

HERE'S WHAT YOU DO

1. Use scissors to cut the shapes of bird's eggs from the construction paper. Glue the eggs onto the cardboard.

2. Glue short strands of yarn under the eggs for a nest. Allow them to dry completely.

3. Use markers to draw tree branches around the nest and speckles on the eggs.

Mother robin redbreast should glue her eggs in a tree, Then her baby birds can stay until they're ninety-three!

MORE ART FUN!

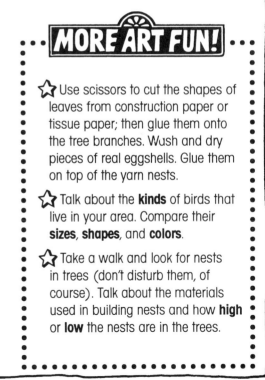

☆ Use scissors to cut the shapes of leaves from construction paper or tissue paper; then glue them onto the tree branches. Wash and dry pieces of real eggshells. Glue them on top of the yarn nests.

☆ Talk about the **kinds** of birds that live in your area. Compare their **sizes**, **shapes**, and **colors**.

☆ Take a walk and look for nests in trees (don't disturb them, of course). Talk about the materials used in building nests and how **high** or **low** the nests are in the trees.

Paper House

Make a house from paper,
leave the front door open wide,
Put faces in the windows
of the folks who live inside!

HERE'S WHAT YOU NEED

White craft glue

Markers

Construction paper
(two sheets, contrasting colors)

Old magazines or photos

Child safety scissors

HERE'S WHAT YOU DO

1 Lay two sheets of construction paper on top of each other. Use scissors to cut out the shape of a house from both sheets of paper.

2 Cut out windows and a front door from one sheet only.

3 Cut out pictures of people's faces from old magazines or photos.

4 Glue together the two houses.

5 Glue people in the windows and doorway of the house. Use markers to add things such as shutters, bricks, and a roof to your house.

CUT

FOLD

CUT

BEND BACK ON FOLD LINES

CUT

FOLD

FOLD

CUT

MAKE A WHOLE TOWN

MORE ART FUN!

☆ Use scissors to cut out house numbers from construction paper. Glue them above the front door.

135

☆ Make a Popsicle stick house. Glue the sticks in the shape of a house onto a piece of cardboard. Use markers to add windows and doors to the house.

☆ Draw a picture of your house at your favorite time of year.

Leaf Prints

*If autumn leaves are falling,
glue them to the ground;
When winter snows are shoveled,
the colors will be found!*

HERE'S WHAT YOU NEED

White craft glue

Leaves

Cardboard

Poster paint

Paint roller

Thin white paper

Styrofoam tray
(from fruits or vegetables)

Newspaper

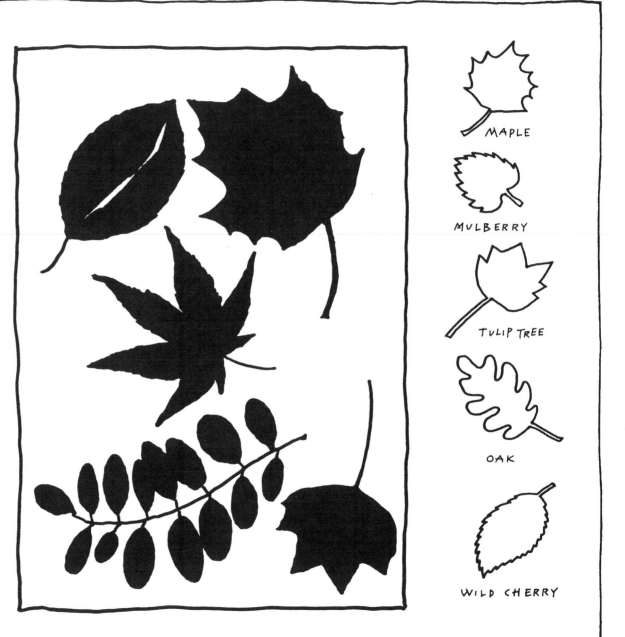

MAPLE

MULBERRY

TULIP TREE

OAK

WILD CHERRY

HERE'S WHAT YOU DO

1 Cover table with newspaper. Pour a small amount of paint into styrofoam tray.

2 Glue leaves onto cardboard, and allow them to dry completely. Move roller back and forth through the paint; then roll over leaves.

3 Lay thin paper over leaves. Rub a hand back and forth over paper. Lift for a leaf print.

MORE ART FUN!

☆ Roll paint onto wire mesh, lace, or netting. Lay paper on top, then lift for prints.

☆ Make up a poem about falling leaves and autumn fun. If you could taste autumn, what would it taste like?

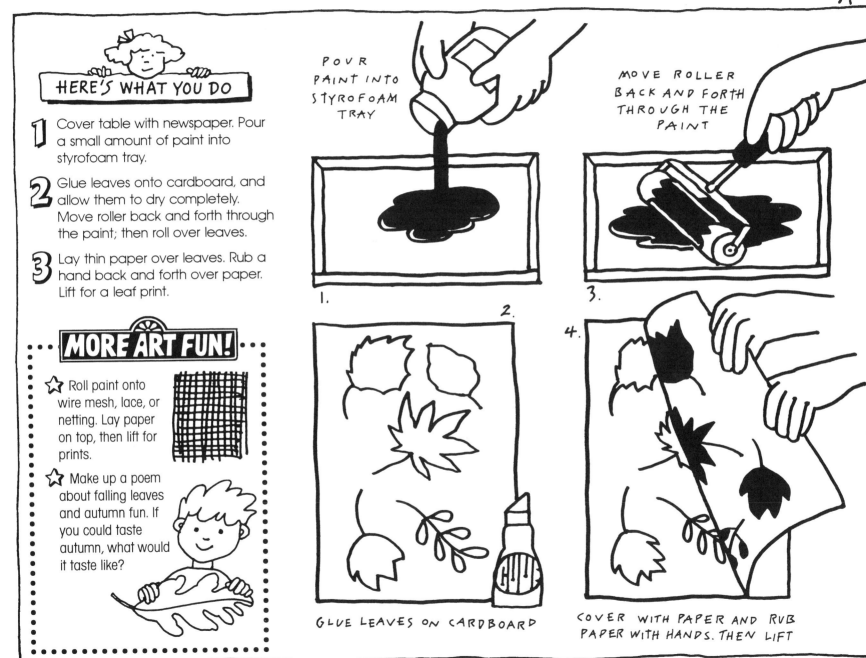

POUR PAINT INTO STYROFOAM TRAY

MOVE ROLLER BACK AND FORTH THROUGH THE PAINT

1.

2.

3.

4.

GLUE LEAVES ON CARDBOARD

COVER WITH PAPER AND RUB PAPER WITH HANDS. THEN LIFT

Paper Bag Puppet

*When it's hard to tell the reasons
why you're having a bad day,
Make a paper bag puppet
and tell it what to say!*

HERE'S WHAT YOU NEED

White craft glue

Small brown paper bag

Construction paper

Yarn

Child safety scissors

Markers

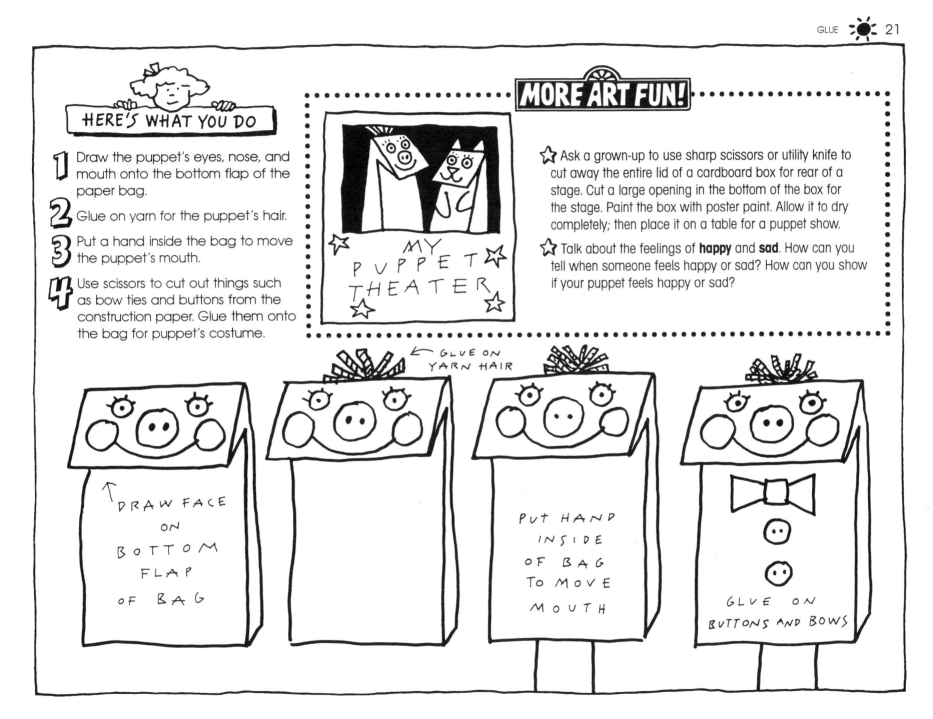

HERE'S WHAT YOU DO

1 Draw the puppet's eyes, nose, and mouth onto the bottom flap of the paper bag.

2 Glue on yarn for the puppet's hair.

3 Put a hand inside the bag to move the puppet's mouth.

4 Use scissors to cut out things such as bow ties and buttons from the construction paper. Glue them onto the bag for puppet's costume.

MORE ART FUN!

MY PUPPET THEATER

☆ Ask a grown-up to use sharp scissors or utility knife to cut away the entire lid of a cardboard box for rear of a stage. Cut a large opening in the bottom of the box for the stage. Paint the box with poster paint. Allow it to dry completely; then place it on a table for a puppet show.

☆ Talk about the feelings of **happy** and **sad**. How can you tell when someone feels happy or sad? How can you show if your puppet feels happy or sad?

GLUE ON YARN HAIR

DRAW FACE ON BOTTOM FLAP OF BAG

PUT HAND INSIDE OF BAG TO MOVE MOUTH

GLUE ON BUTTONS AND BOWS

Funny Hats

When you need a special hat,
don't buy it in a shop,
Make it from scrap paper,
and glue a feather at the top!

HERE'S WHAT YOU NEED

White craft glue

Construction paper

Markers

Stapler

Child safety scissors

Feather

Ribbon

HERE'S WHAT YOU DO

1 Use scissors to cut a large circle from construction paper.

2 Use markers to draw on the circle.

3 Make a single cut from the outside edge of the circle into the center. Overlap edges of circle; then staple together for a peaked hat.

4 Staple a length of ribbon onto both sides of hat to tie under the chin.

5 Glue the feather poking out the top of the hat.

CIRCLE CENTER

← CUT

CUT OUT CIRCLE

ATTACH FEATHER

STAPLE TOGETHER

DECORATE WITH MARKERS

STAPLE RIBBON ON BOTH SIDES

MORE ART FUN!

☆ Glue things such as artificial or tissue paper flowers, scrap fabric trim, sequins, and pom-poms onto the hat.

☆ Look through old magazines for kinds of special hats people wear – football helmets, wedding veils, baseball caps. Cut some out of magazines and glue on a piece of paper for a crazy hat collage.

FOOTBALL   BRIDE   BASEBALL

ABE LINCOLN   COWBOY   COOK

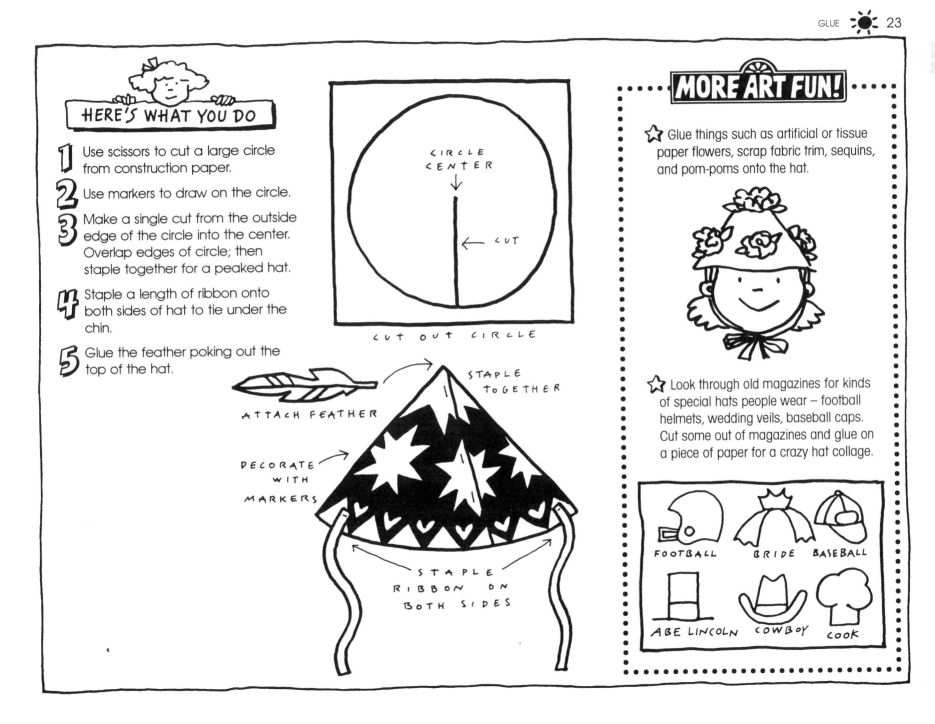

Paper Plate Spider

Make a creepy spider,
glue on legs so it can crawl,
Then sneak up on your friends
and ask what's on the wall!

HERE'S WHAT YOU NEED

White craft glue

Small white paper plate

Black construction paper

Black marker

Long piece of string

Child safety scissors

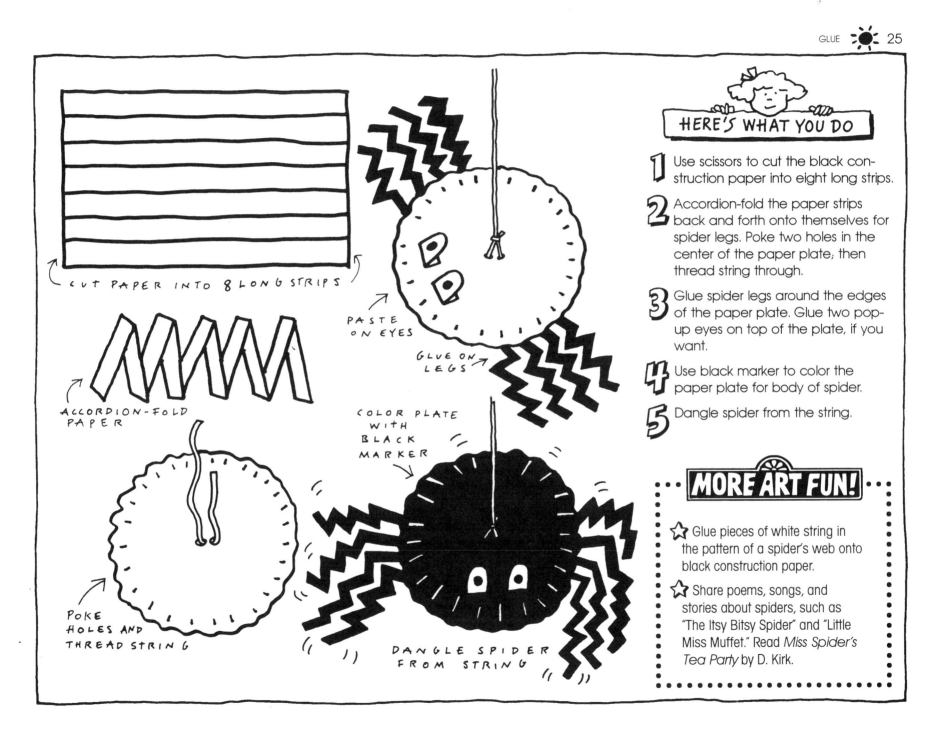

CUT PAPER INTO 8 LONG STRIPS

ACCORDION-FOLD PAPER

POKE HOLES AND THREAD STRING

PASTE ON EYES

GLUE ON LEGS

COLOR PLATE WITH BLACK MARKER

DANGLE SPIDER FROM STRING

HERE'S WHAT YOU DO

1 Use scissors to cut the black construction paper into eight long strips.

2 Accordion-fold the paper strips back and forth onto themselves for spider legs. Poke two holes in the center of the paper plate; then thread string through.

3 Glue spider legs around the edges of the paper plate. Glue two pop-up eyes on top of the plate, if you want.

4 Use black marker to color the paper plate for body of spider.

5 Dangle spider from the string.

MORE ART FUN!

☆ Glue pieces of white string in the pattern of a spider's web onto black construction paper.

☆ Share poems, songs, and stories about spiders, such as "The Itsy Bitsy Spider" and "Little Miss Muffet." Read *Miss Spider's Tea Party* by D. Kirk.

Salt Shaker Sand

*In the middle of the winter,
just forget the snow and sleet,
Make a sandy beach,
then feel it with your feet!*

HERE'S WHAT YOU NEED

White craft glue

Salt shaker

Shirt cardboard

Pasta shells

Newspaper

Small bowl

Paintbrush

HERE'S WHAT YOU DO

1 Pour glue into bowl; then dilute it with a few drops of water.

2 Working over newspaper, brush glue onto the shirt cardboard.

3 Sprinkle salt onto the cardboard (catch excess salt on newspaper).

4 Glue pasta shells onto the salted cardboard.

MORE ART FUN!

☆ Add a few drops of food color to the salt for colored sand.

☆ Glue pasta shells onto cardboard. Allow to dry completely; then paint shells with poster paint.

☆ Visit a pet store and look at snails and hermit crabs.

☆ Look in a book of shells and pick out the **biggest**, the **smallest** – plus the one you like the best!

Button-Down Cardboard Shirt

*Buttons are smooth and round,
as they line up in a row,
Grab a bunch and glue them on,
there's no need to sew!*

HERE'S WHAT YOU NEED

White craft glue

Construction paper

Shirt cardboard

Markers

Child safety scissors

Assorted flat buttons

(Caution: Do not use buttons with young children who may put them in their mouths.)

HERE'S WHAT YOU DO

1. Use scissors to cut the shape of a shirt collar from construction paper.

2. Glue collar onto the top half of the cardboard for a shirt.

3. Use markers to draw patterns onto the shirt.

4. Glue a row of buttons down the front of the shirt.

MORE ART FUN!

☆ Use scissors to cut out a tie from construction paper (or fabric). Glue the tie onto the shirt; then use markers to color paper tie.

☆ Describe your favorite piece of clothing and how you feel when you wear it.

Milk Carton Caboose

*When you're done eating breakfast
and the last milk drop's been poured,
Glue wheels onto the empty carton,
then call out "all aboard!"*

HERE'S WHAT YOU NEED

White craft glue

Milk carton
(pint, quart, or half gallon)

White paper

Tape

Recycled aluminum foil

Child safety scissors

Markers

Shirt cardboard

HERE'S WHAT YOU DO

1 Rinse out milk carton and press the top flap down. Tape shut.

2 Use white paper and tape to wrap the carton.

3 Use scissors to cut out four circles from the cardboard.

4 Cover the cardboard in foil; then glue onto sides of the carton for wheels.

5 Use markers to add things such as windows and doors for your train.

MORE ART FUN!

☆ Make additional train cars; then attach string between each car to hold them together. Glue Popsicle sticks onto cardboard for train tracks.

☆ Read *The Little Red Caboose* by Marian Potter.

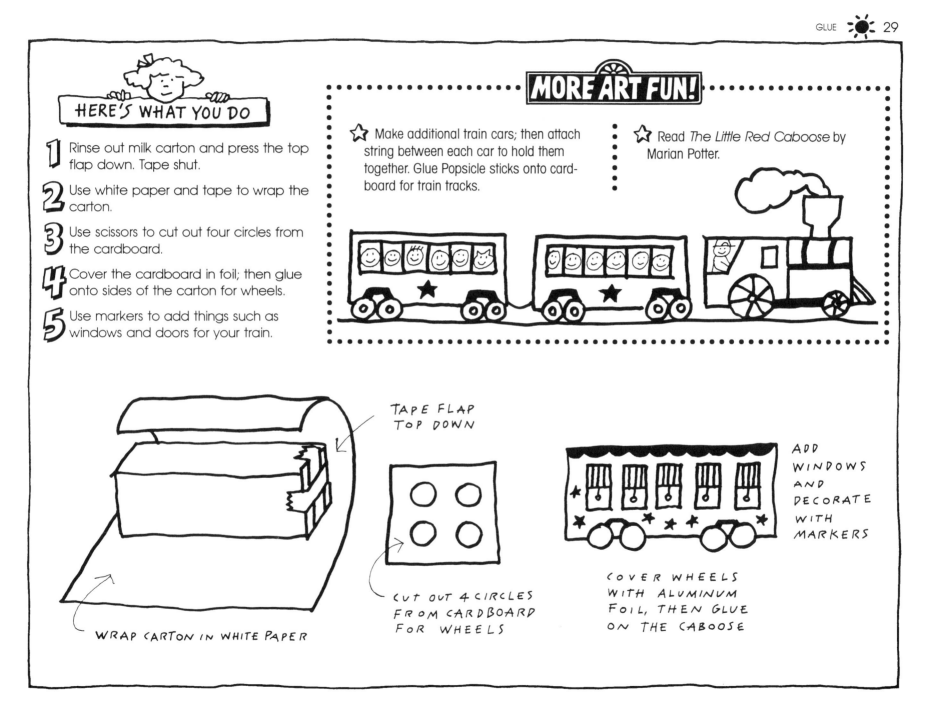

TAPE FLAP TOP DOWN

WRAP CARTON IN WHITE PAPER

CUT OUT 4 CIRCLES FROM CARDBOARD FOR WHEELS

ADD WINDOWS AND DECORATE WITH MARKERS

COVER WHEELS WITH ALUMINUM FOIL, THEN GLUE ON THE CABOOSE

Egg Carton Caterpillar

A caterpillar crawls on trees,
finding leaves to eat,
Make one from an egg carton
and glue on lots of feet!

HERE'S WHAT YOU NEED

White craft glue

Cardboard egg carton

Shirt cardboard

Pipe cleaner

Child safety scissors

Poster paint

Paintbrush

HERE'S WHAT YOU DO

1 Use scissors to cut off the egg carton lid. Cut the carton in half the long way.

2 Cut the shirt cardboard into six strips — long enough to stick out from underneath both sides of the carton's compartments.

3 Turn the carton over and glue the cardboard strips across the underside of each compartment for caterpillar's legs.

4 Poke two short pieces of pipe cleaner into top of the first compartment for the caterpillar's antennae.

5 Paint the caterpillar with poster paints.

MORE ART FUN!

☆ Use scissors to cut out the shape of a butterfly from the egg carton's lid. Paint the butterfly with poster paint; then glue on a pipe cleaner for butterfly's antennae.

☆ Read *The Very Hungry Caterpillar* by Eric Carle.

☆ Talk about how animals and people change in their lives.

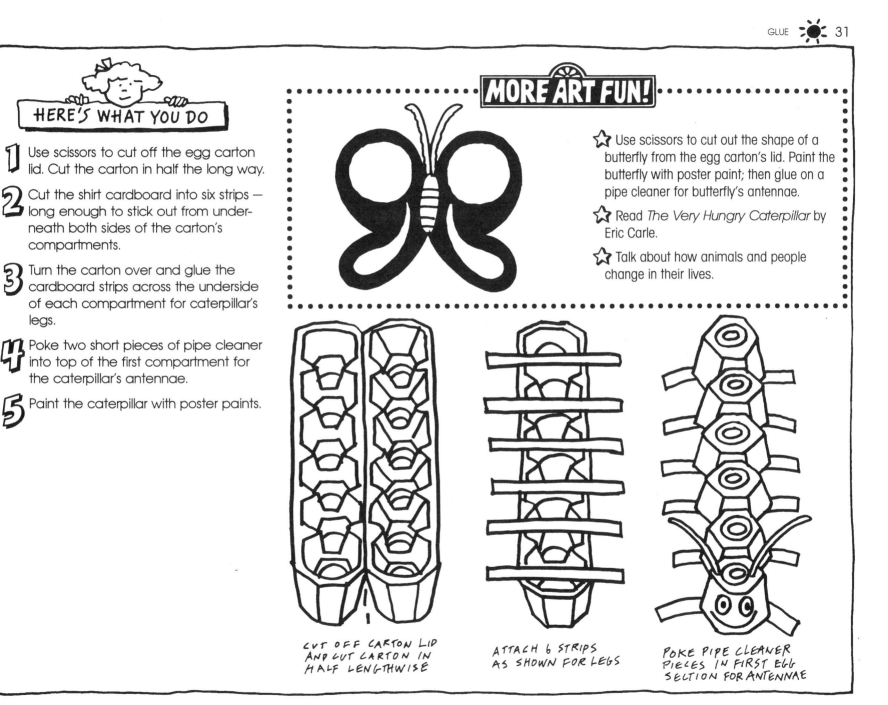

CUT OFF CARTON LID AND CUT CARTON IN HALF LENGTHWISE

ATTACH 6 STRIPS AS SHOWN FOR LEGS

POKE PIPE CLEANER PIECES IN FIRST EGG SECTION FOR ANTENNAE

Paper Cars

Wheels are circles spinning 'round,
they go from here to there,
What a bumpy ride we'd have,
if their shape were square!

HERE'S WHAT YOU NEED

White craft glue

Cardboard

Construction paper

Pasta wheels

Markers

Child safety scissors

HERE'S WHAT YOU DO

1 Use scissors to cut out shapes of cars from construction paper. Glue cars onto the cardboard.

2 Use a big glob of glue to attach the pasta wheels to the cars. Allow them to dry completely.

3 Use markers to draw street signs, roads, and traffic lights onto the cardboard.

MORE ART FUN!

☆ Glue cars onto a sheet of black paper for a nighttime road scene. Use scissors to cut highway lights from construction paper or foil; then glue onto black paper.

☆ Draw the different **shapes** that road signs come in. Do you know what each sign means?

STOP

Picture Frame

HERE'S WHAT YOU DO

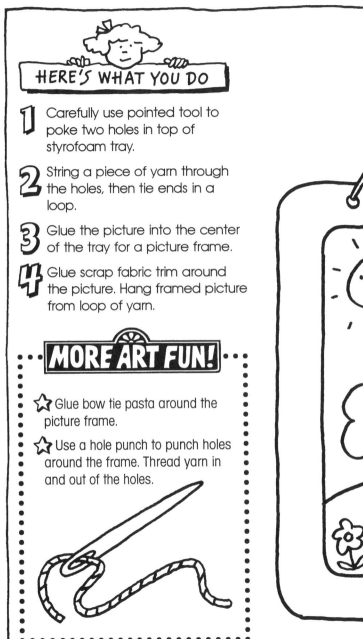

1 Carefully use pointed tool to poke two holes in top of styrofoam tray.

2 String a piece of yarn through the holes, then tie ends in a loop.

3 Glue the picture into the center of the tray for a picture frame.

4 Glue scrap fabric trim around the picture. Hang framed picture from loop of yarn.

MORE ART FUN!

☆ Glue bow tie pasta around the picture frame.

☆ Use a hole punch to punch holes around the frame. Thread yarn in and out of the holes.

When it's time to clean up art supplies, put your painting in a frame, Proudly hang it in a special place, and don't forget to sign your name!

HERE'S WHAT YOU NEED

White craft glue

Styrofoam tray (from fruit or vegetables)

Picture (small enough to fit in center of tray)

Yarn

Scrap fabric trim

*Pointed tool

Wooden Sculpture

*Build a tower of wooden blocks —
it can be as tall as you,
It won't even topple over,
if you stack it up with glue!*

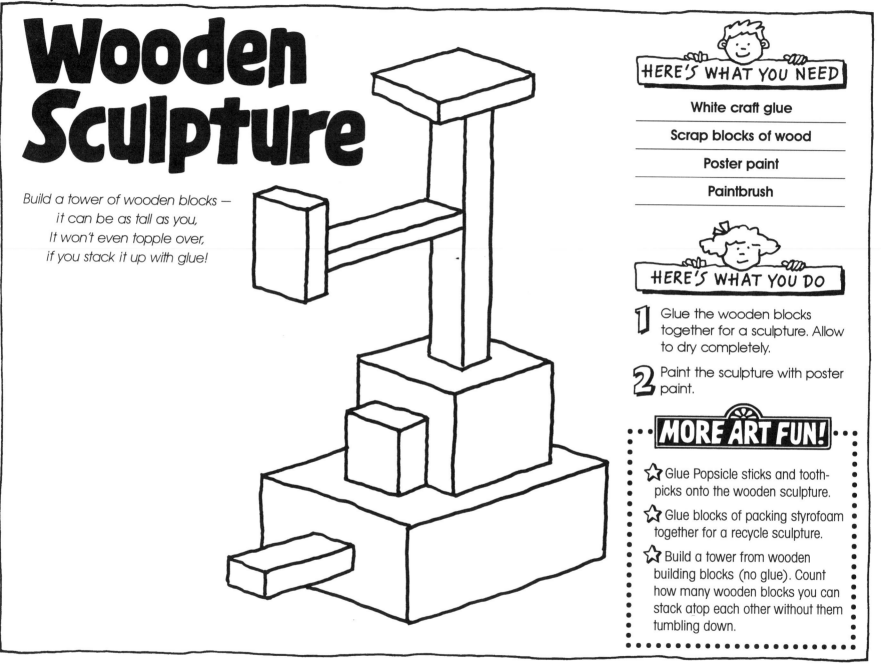

White craft glue

Scrap blocks of wood

Poster paint

Paintbrush

HERE'S WHAT YOU DO

1 Glue the wooden blocks together for a sculpture. Allow to dry completely.

2 Paint the sculpture with poster paint.

MORE ART FUN!

☆ Glue Popsicle sticks and toothpicks onto the wooden sculpture.

☆ Glue blocks of packing styrofoam together for a recycle sculpture.

☆ Build a tower from wooden building blocks (no glue). Count how many wooden blocks you can stack atop each other without them tumbling down.

PAPER

Paper can be smooth or rough,
you can hang it on a wall,
It can be cut and colored
or crumpled in a ball!

Paper Bowl Turtles

*Turtles move so slowly
but you don't have to wait,
Make one with a marker
and a paper plate!*

HERE'S WHAT YOU NEED

Small white paper bowl

Shirt cardboard

White craft glue

Child safety scissors

Markers (green and black)

HERE'S WHAT YOU DO

1 Use scissors to cut the turtle's legs, head, and tail from shirt cardboard. Turn the bowl upside down and glue them to the underside rim.

2 Use markers to color the turtle.

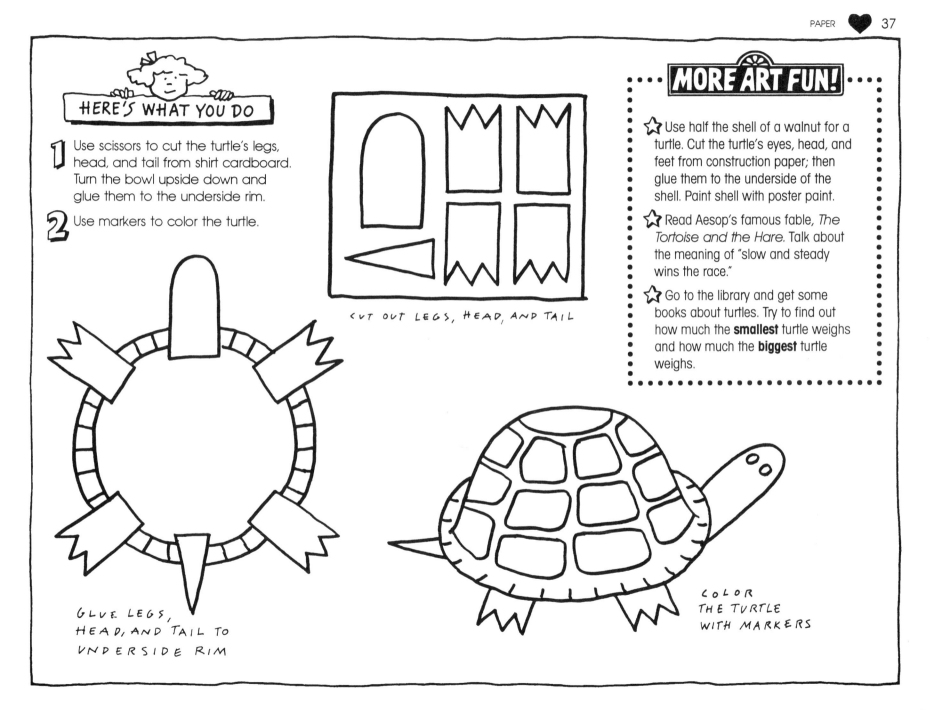

CUT OUT LEGS, HEAD, AND TAIL

GLUE LEGS, HEAD, AND TAIL TO UNDERSIDE RIM

COLOR THE TURTLE WITH MARKERS

MORE ART FUN!

☆ Use half the shell of a walnut for a turtle. Cut the turtle's eyes, head, and feet from construction paper; then glue them to the underside of the shell. Paint shell with poster paint.

☆ Read Aesop's famous fable, *The Tortoise and the Hare.* Talk about the meaning of "slow and steady wins the race."

☆ Go to the library and get some books about turtles. Try to find out how much the **smallest** turtle weighs and how much the **biggest** turtle weighs.

Traffic Lights

Color three paper plates and pretend you're a traffic cop, Yellow means the cars slow down, green they go, and red they stop!

HERE'S WHAT YOU NEED

Small white paper plates (3)

Cardboard paper towel tube

**Poster paint
(red, yellow, and green)**

Paintbrush

Child safety scissors

White craft glue

Newspaper

HERE'S WHAT YOU DO

1. Cover table with newspaper. Use scissors to cut out center circle from the paper plate.

2. Paint one paper plate center red, another yellow, and a third green. Allow them to dry completely.

3. Glue plates onto cardboard tube for a traffic light.

MORE ART FUN!

☆ Use scissors to cut out the shape of a police officer's badge from shirt cardboard; then wrap it in recycled aluminum foil. Tape a safety pin on the back of the badge and wear it on a shirt.

☆ Invite a police officer to come to your preschool or school. Ask him or her a lot of questions about what an officer does all day. Would you like to be a police officer someday?

Flying Flags

*It's fun to march and wave up high,
a paper flag you've made,
When people see you passing by,
they'll think you're in a parade!*

HERE'S WHAT YOU NEED

Construction paper

Cardboard tube from paper towel roll

White craft glue

Child safety scissors

Tape

HERE'S WHAT YOU DO

1 Use scissors to cut the shape of a flag from construction paper.

2 Cut designs such as flowers, letters, or numbers from scraps of construction paper.

3 Glue paper designs onto flag.

4 Use tape to attach outer edge of flag to the cardboard tube.

MORE ART FUN!

☆ Cut the shape of a flag from scrap fabric. Use iron-ons, fabric trim, and fabric paint to decorate flag. Staple or glue edge of flag to a dowel rod.

☆ Make some flags to celebrate a holiday or a special birthday. Then, put on some John Philip Sousa marching music and parade around the house.

Weaving Paper

*Weaving paper's so much fun
you won't ever want to stop,
Go underneath the first strip,
then right over the top!*

HERE'S WHAT YOU NEED

**Construction paper
(2 different-colored sheets the
same size)**

Child safety scissors

HERE'S WHAT YOU DO

1 Use scissors to cut one sheet of paper into strips. Fold the other sheet of paper in half.

2 Starting at the fold, cut slits across the paper, stopping about one inch (2.5 cm) from the edge. Lay the paper flat.

3 Weave strips of paper in and out of the slits. First over one slit, then under the next slit, through to the other side.

4 Repeat with the next strip, starting under the slit, then going over. Alternate each strip until paper is completely woven.

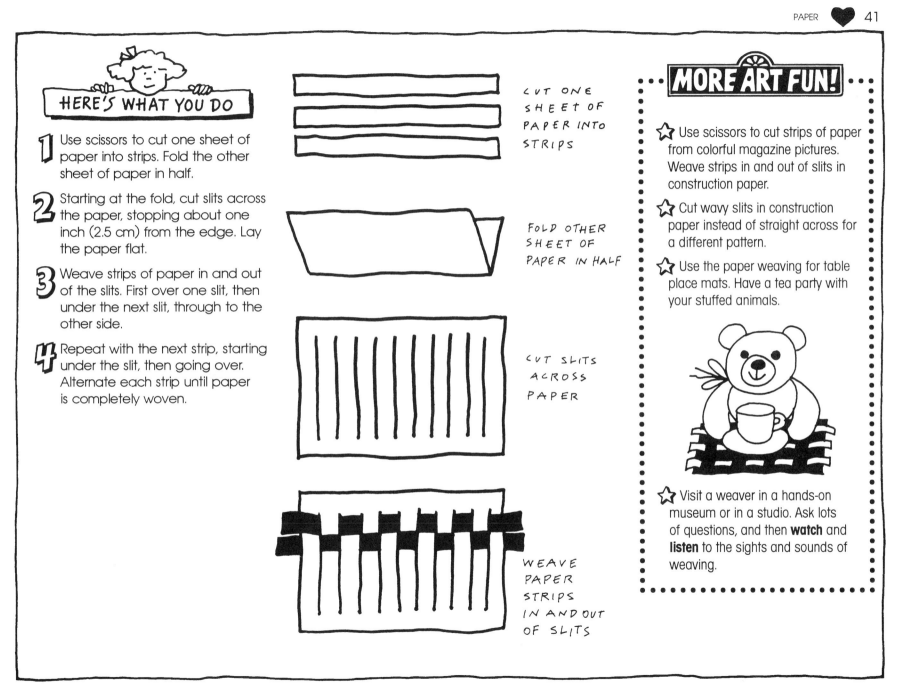

CUT ONE SHEET OF PAPER INTO STRIPS

FOLD OTHER SHEET OF PAPER IN HALF

CUT SLITS ACROSS PAPER

WEAVE PAPER STRIPS IN AND OUT OF SLITS

MORE ART FUN!

☆ Use scissors to cut strips of paper from colorful magazine pictures. Weave strips in and out of slits in construction paper.

☆ Cut wavy slits in construction paper instead of straight across for a different pattern.

☆ Use the paper weaving for table place mats. Have a tea party with your stuffed animals.

☆ Visit a weaver in a hands-on museum or in a studio. Ask lots of questions, and then **watch** and **listen** to the sights and sounds of weaving.

Paper Dolls

*Cut rows of dolls from paper,
then stand them end to end,
They hold on to each other,
just like they're best of friends!*

HERE'S WHAT YOU NEED

Sheet of paper

Child safety scissors

Pencil

Markers

HERE'S WHAT YOU DO

1 Fold the paper lengthwise in fourths. Use the pencil to draw the shape of a figure on the top fold of paper (make sure drawing touches folds on both sides in at least one place).

2 Use scissors to cut out the figure, keeping folded edges intact in several places on the drawing.

3 Open the paper for a row of dolls.

4 Use markers to draw things such as clothing, hair, and a face on each paper doll.

☆ Glue rows of paper dolls onto construction paper. Use scissors to cut out shapes such as trees, flowers, or animals from construction paper.

☆ Talk about how people from other cultures dress. Then, draw clothes from other lands on your paper dolls as they hold hands around the world.

FOLD PAPER IN FOURTHS

DRAW FIGURE ON FIRST FOLD

OPEN PAPER AND DECORATE DOLLS

Paper Plate Mask

*Want to look like someone,
who's come from outer space,
Wear a mask of paper plates
to cover up your face!*

HERE'S WHAT YOU NEED

White paper plate

Cardboard tube
from paper towel roll

Child safety scissors

White craft glue

Construction paper

Stapler

Markers

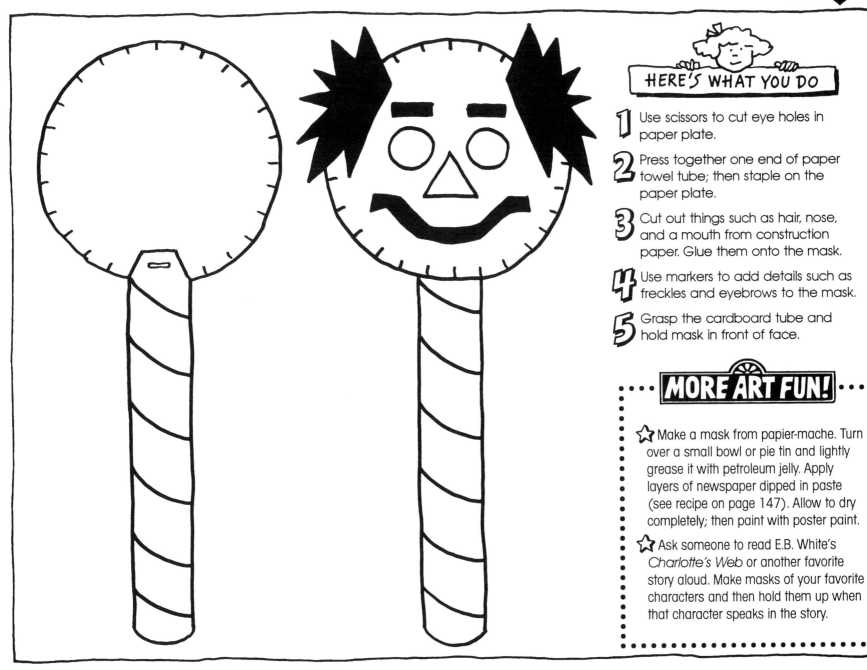

HERE'S WHAT YOU DO

1. Use scissors to cut eye holes in paper plate.

2. Press together one end of paper towel tube; then staple on the paper plate.

3. Cut out things such as hair, nose, and a mouth from construction paper. Glue them onto the mask.

4. Use markers to add details such as freckles and eyebrows to the mask.

5. Grasp the cardboard tube and hold mask in front of face.

MORE ART FUN!

☆ Make a mask from papier-mache. Turn over a small bowl or pie tin and lightly grease it with petroleum jelly. Apply layers of newspaper dipped in paste (see recipe on page 147). Allow to dry completely; then paint with poster paint.

☆ Ask someone to read E.B. White's *Charlotte's Web* or another favorite story aloud. Make masks of your favorite characters and then hold them up when that character speaks in the story.

Puddle Art

*When paint drips on paper
fold it closed, then open wide,
You'll see the dots on one half
jump to the other side!*

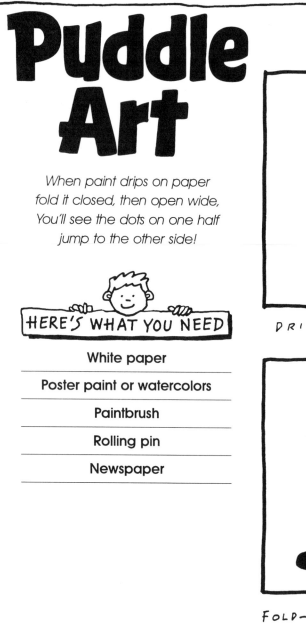

HERE'S WHAT YOU NEED

White paper

Poster paint or watercolors

Paintbrush

Rolling pin

Newspaper

DRIP PAINT ON ONE HALF OF FOLDED PAPER

FOLD—PRESS PAPER TOGETHER—THEN OPEN IT UP

HERE'S WHAT YOU DO

1 Cover table with newspaper. Fold white paper in half.

2 Drip small puddles of paint onto one-half of the paper; then fold it closed.

3 Use rolling pin to go back and forth over top of paper.

4 Open paper for a double design.

MORE ART FUN!

☆ Open your puddle art and show it to friends. What does everyone think it looks like – a flower? a cat? a bird? What do you think it looks like? If you add details (like cat whiskers) with markers, does it begin to take on a definite shape?

☆ Use scissors to cut paper into shapes such as a butterfly, heart, or circle. Fold in half and drip paint on one side. Rub back and forth over top; then open for double design.

Funny Fingerprints

*When something's in the garden
eating all that it can find,
Lay down a piece of paper
so it can leave its prints behind!*

HERE'S WHAT YOU NEED

Sheet of paper

Poster paint

Sponge

Plastic margarine tub

Markers (fine point)

Child safety scissors

Newspaper

HERE'S WHAT YOU DO

1. Cover table with newspaper. Use scissors to cut sponge to fit inside plastic margarine tub. Saturate sponge with paint for a printing pad.

2. Press fingertip into pad; then press onto paper for fingerprints.

3. Use markers to draw things such as funny people, little animals, and silly insects on fingerprints.

MORE ART FUN!

☆ Working outdoors, use printing pad made from a large sponge. Press a bare foot or hand on pad, then onto paper for footprint or handprint.

☆ Make fingerprint stationery or party invitations. Use pale-colored paper or bright-colored paint to draw funny creatures across paper. Having a picnic? How about paper with a family of ants traipsing across the invitation!

Paper Moon & Stars

To reach the sky, fly paper kites
high above the trees,
Then hang a paper moon and stars,
and drift down on a breeze!

HERE'S WHAT YOU NEED

Construction paper
(dark blue or black)

Paper plate

Recycled aluminum foil

Styrofoam packing pellets
(recycled)

Marker (black)

White craft glue

Child safety scissors

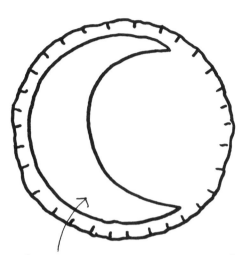

CUT MOON SHAPE OUT OF PLATE

CUT STAR SHAPES OUT OF FOIL

HERE'S WHAT YOU DO

1 Use scissors to cut a moon shape from the paper plate.

2 Cut stars out from aluminum foil.

3 Glue packing pellets onto one side of paper plate moon.

4 Wrap moon in foil, and press down around bumps. Use black marker to draw around bumps for moon's shadows.

5 Glue moon and stars onto construction paper for a night sky.

GLUE PELLETS ON MOON SHAPE. THEN WRAP THE MOON IN FOIL

GLUE MOON AND STARS ON DARK BLUE CONSTRUCTION PAPER

MORE ART FUN!

☆ Draw clouds and moonlit shapes onto the construction paper with white chalk.

☆ Read Margaret Wise Brown's *Good Night, Moon.*

☆ Stay up late on a moonlit night. Ask a grown-up to take you for a walk and look at the shape of the moon and twinkling stars. Is the night sky black or blue or purple?

Snowflake Decoration

If stars came down from the sky,
how beautiful it would be,
If they landed on pine branches,
to decorate a tree!

HERE'S WHAT YOU NEED

Sheet of square paper

Child safety scissors

Pine tree branch

Container
(large enough to hold branch)

Recycled aluminum foil

String, yarn, or florist's wire

Hole punch

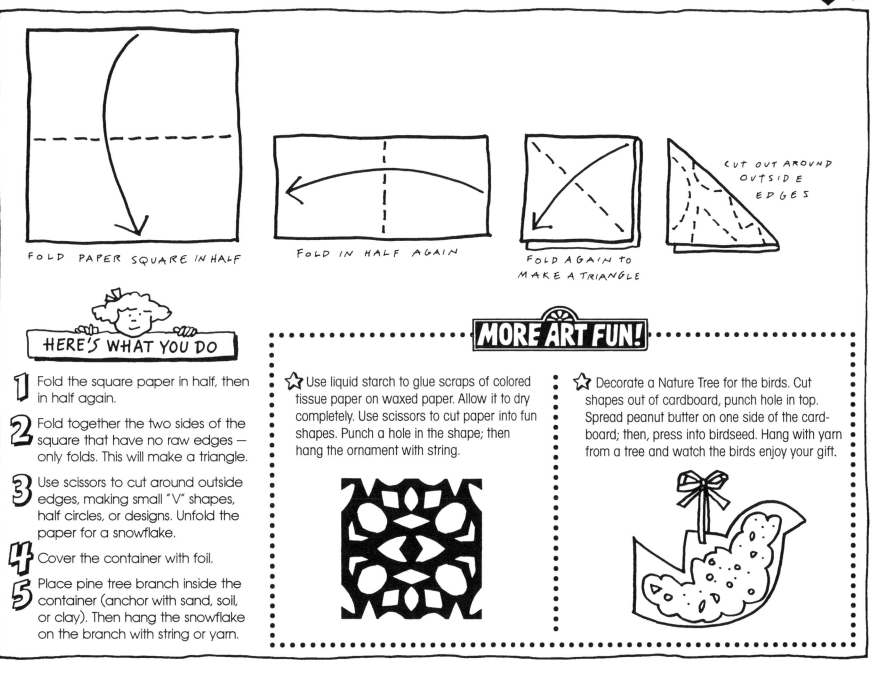

FOLD PAPER SQUARE IN HALF

FOLD IN HALF AGAIN

FOLD AGAIN TO MAKE A TRIANGLE

CUT OUT AROUND OUTSIDE EDGES

HERE'S WHAT YOU DO

1 Fold the square paper in half, then in half again.

2 Fold together the two sides of the square that have no raw edges — only folds. This will make a triangle.

3 Use scissors to cut around outside edges, making small "V" shapes, half circles, or designs. Unfold the paper for a snowflake.

4 Cover the container with foil.

5 Place pine tree branch inside the container (anchor with sand, soil, or clay). Then hang the snowflake on the branch with string or yarn.

MORE ART FUN!

☆ Use liquid starch to glue scraps of colored tissue paper on waxed paper. Allow it to dry completely. Use scissors to cut paper into fun shapes. Punch a hole in the shape; then hang the ornament with string.

☆ Decorate a Nature Tree for the birds. Cut shapes out of cardboard, punch hole in top. Spread peanut butter on one side of the cardboard; then, press into birdseed. Hang with yarn from a tree and watch the birds enjoy your gift.

Cardboard Mittens

Would you like some mittens you won't ever have to mend? Make them out of cardboard, then wear them for pretend!

HERE'S WHAT YOU NEED

Shirt cardboard

Child safety scissors

Pencil

Markers

Yarn

HERE'S WHAT YOU DO

1. Spread each hand out flat on the cardboard, then trace around it with the pencil.

2. Use scissors to cut out hands for mittens.

3. Poke a hole in top of each mitten, and tie the ends of a long strand of yarn through the hole (yarn should drape around neck and shoulders).

4. Use markers to draw designs on mittens.

MORE ART FUN!

☆ Glue scraps of fabric and yarn onto the mittens.

☆ Act out the poem "The Three Little Kittens Who Lost Their Mittens." Glue whiskers made from black construction paper on your face to look like kittens.

☆ Find all your stray mittens. See if you can make pairs out of them. The **colors** and **patterns** can be different, but you'll need one for the **right hand** and one for the **left hand** to make a pair.

Paper Mosaic

HERE'S WHAT YOU NEED

Construction paper
(assorted colors)

Shirt cardboard

Paper plates

Paintbrush

White craft glue

Pencil

Child safety scissors

MORE ART FUN!

☆ Use scissors to cut colorful magazine pictures into small pieces; then glue down onto cardboard for a mosaic.

☆ Tear pieces of tissue paper and glue onto a piece of waxed paper. Hang in a sunny window for a stained-glass mosaic.

☆ Visit a church with stained-glass windows on a sunny day.

*Clean-up is no problem
for a kangaroo,
Scraps go in its pocket
when it's sure it's through!*

HERE'S WHAT YOU DO

1 Use scissors to cut construction paper into small pieces. Separate them by color and place the pieces onto paper plates.

2 Cut shirt cardboard in half (it's easier to work on a small piece of cardboard, as mosaic takes time and patience).

3 Thin the glue by adding a few drops of water.

4 Use pencil to lightly draw a design onto cardboard.

5 Use the paintbrush to glue a small area of the design at a time. Glue pieces of paper one at a time onto the design, for a colorful mosaic.

Paper Plate Fish

*Bright, shiny fish
swim in schools across the bay,
As they tire of one place,
they simply swim away!*

Small white paper plate

Watercolor paint

Paintbrush

Container of water

Construction paper
(blue, green, or white)

White craft glue

Markers

Child safety scissors

HERE'S WHAT YOU DO

1. Use scissors to cut out the shape of a fish from the paper plate.

2. Paint the fish with watercolor paint, and allow to dry completely.

3. Use markers to add things such as eyes, scales, and gills to the fish.

4. Glue fish onto construction paper.

5. Paint things such as underwater plants and sea creatures onto construction paper.

PAPER PLATE

CUT OUT FISH SHAPE

MORE ART FUN!

☆ Glue fish into the center of a styrofoam tray (from fruits or vegetables). Stretch clear plastic wrap across front of tray, and tape in place for a fish tank.

☆ Decorate your paper plate with bits of tissue paper. For a bright and shiny fish, glue on glitter, too.

☆ Visit an aquarium or a pet shop to see brightly colored fish.

PAINT THE FISH

ADD EYES, SCALES, AND GILLS

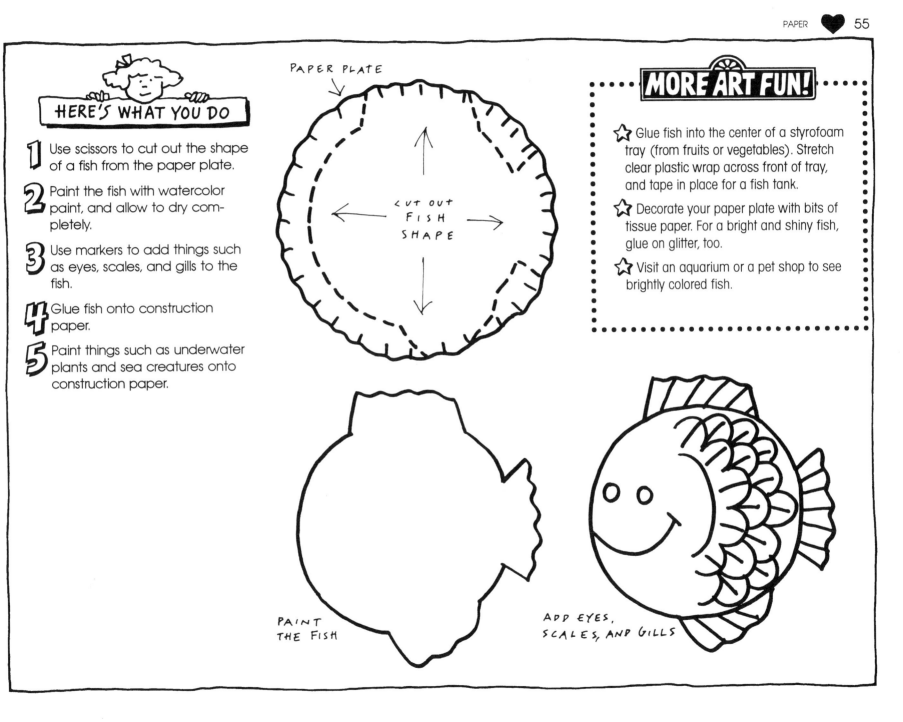

Cardboard Stand-Ups

*If you need paper
that's stiff and heavyweight,
Use a piece of cardboard,
'cause it will stand up straight!*

HERE'S WHAT YOU NEED

Shirt cardboard

Child safety scissors

Pencil

Markers

HERE'S WHAT YOU DO

1 Fold the shirt cardboard in half.

2 Use a pencil to draw things such as cars, trucks, houses, or animals onto cardboard (top of drawing should run along the cardboard fold).

3 Use scissors to cut out the drawing (make sure not to cut into the fold) for two identical objects joined together along the top fold.

4 Use markers to color the cardboard cutout on both sides.

5 Spread two bottom edges of cutout slightly apart, so it will stand upright.

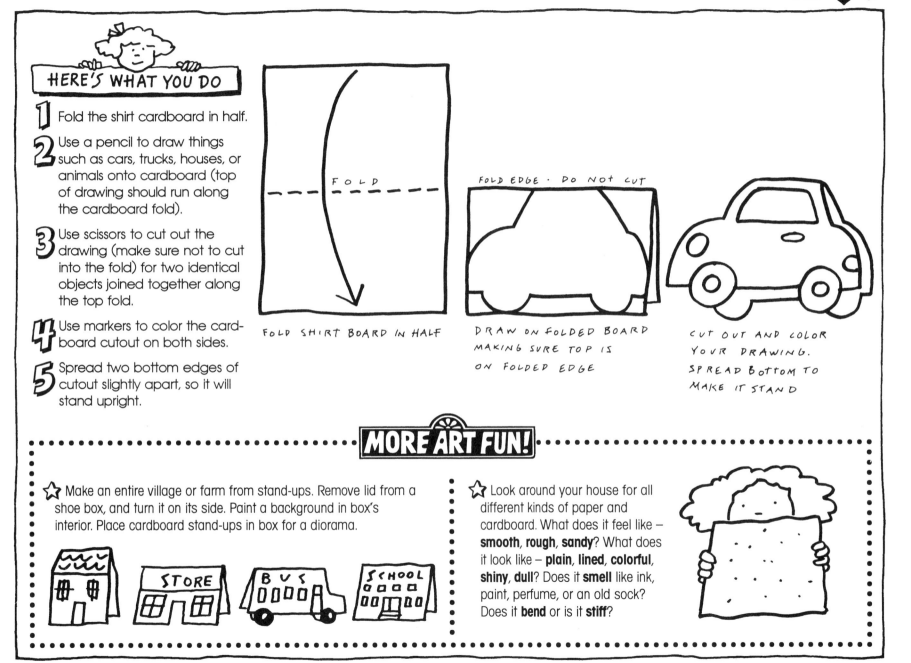

FOLD SHIRT BOARD IN HALF

DRAW ON FOLDED BOARD MAKING SURE TOP IS ON FOLDED EDGE

CUT OUT AND COLOR YOUR DRAWING. SPREAD BOTTOM TO MAKE IT STAND

MORE ART FUN!

☆ Make an entire village or farm from stand-ups. Remove lid from a shoe box, and turn it on its side. Paint a background in box's interior. Place cardboard stand-ups in box for a diorama.

☆ Look around your house for all different kinds of paper and cardboard. What does it feel like – **smooth, rough, sandy**? What does it look like – **plain, lined, colorful, shiny, dull**? Does it **smell** like ink, paint, perfume, or an old sock? Does it **bend** or is it **stiff**?

Paper Plate Face

*Make a face from paper plates
divided into three,
It has eyes and a mouth,
and looks like you or me!*

HERE'S WHAT YOU NEED

**Paper dinner plate
(divided into three sections)**

**Construction paper (red and
blue)**

Child safety scissors

Markers

White craft glue

HERE'S WHAT YOU DO

1 Use scissors to cut shape of largest section of plate from red construction paper. Cut out shapes of the two smaller sections from blue paper.

2 Glue red paper into large section of plate for mouth, then glue blue paper into two smaller sections for eyes.

3 Use markers or scraps of paper to add things such as eyebrows and teeth to puppet's face.

MORE ART FUN!

☆ Use scissors to cut things such as a bow tie, ears, and a hat from construction paper. Glue them onto the plate for a clown's face.

BOW TIE

MAKE 2 EARS

HAT

☆ Look at the shapes of different faces. Are they **round**, **long** (oval like an egg), **square**, or almost **triangle**-shaped?

USE 3-SECTION PAPER PLATE

CUT PAPER AND GLUE IN SECTIONS

BLUE   BLUE

RED

DRAW PUPPET FACE

figure Cutouts

Wondering how tall you are?
Well, here's a way to tell,
Trace yourself on paper,
Then you'll see very well!

HERE'S WHAT YOU DO

1 Use scissors to cut a length of paper five feet (1.5 m) long. Attach it to the floor with tape. Lie down on paper and ask someone to draw around your body with crayon. Cut figure out from paper.

2 Place figure on newspaper spread out on the floor. Use poster paint to paint the paper figure.

MORE ART FUN!

☆ Pose body on the paper in different positions, such as sideways, running, or dancing. Cut out figure and paint with poster paint.

☆ Use scissors to cut out pictures from old magazines that reflect interests of person posing such as sports and hobbies. Glue pictures onto the paper figure for a personal statement.

☆ Cut a double length of paper and lie down on double thickness. Trace and cut out through both layers. Staple together leaving a wide opening. Paint and then stuff with newspaper for a three-dimensional figure.

Magic Wand

*If you need a fairy princess
and one just can't be found,
Sprinkle magic glitter dust
and wave a wand around!*

HERE'S WHAT YOU NEED

Newspaper

Recycled aluminum foil

Crepe paper

Tape

White craft glue

Cardboard

Markers

Child safety scissors

HERE'S WHAT YOU DO

1 Roll three sheets of newspaper together widthwise for a wand; then tape together.

2 Wrap wand in foil, and secure with tape.

3 Use scissors to cut out the shape of a star from cardboard.

4 Cut long strips of crepe paper for streamers.

5 Use markers to color both sides of the star. Glue the star and streamers onto the top of the wand.

MORE ART FUN!

☆ Use scissors to cut a band of construction paper long enough to fit around the head. Cut out stars from shirt cardboard and wrap them in foil. Glue stars onto the band; then tape the band together for a crown.

☆ Tell fairy tales where a fairy princess, prince, or godmother does something magical. Or, make up your own magical story.

PAINT

*Paint a picture in bright colors,
when it's a rainy day,
A yellow sun in the sky
will chase the clouds away!*

Rainbows

*If you want to catch a rainbow,
and you can't reach to the sky,
Paint a picture in every color,
and hang it way up high!*

HERE'S WHAT YOU NEED

Watercolor paint

Paintbrush

Container of water

Sheet of white paper

Markers

Newspaper

Child safety scissors

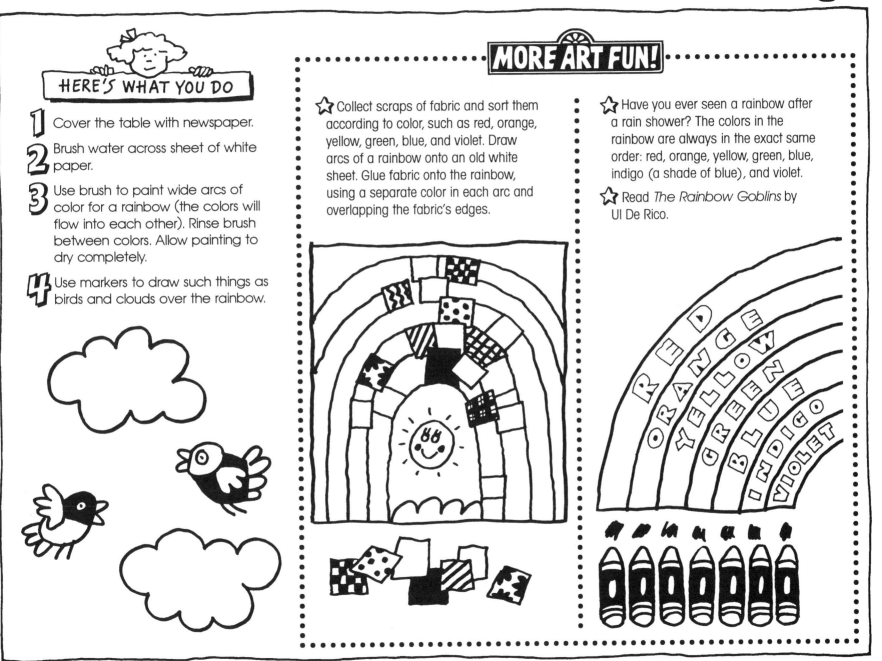

HERE'S WHAT YOU DO

1 Cover the table with newspaper.

2 Brush water across sheet of white paper.

3 Use brush to paint wide arcs of color for a rainbow (the colors will flow into each other). Rinse brush between colors. Allow painting to dry completely.

4 Use markers to draw such things as birds and clouds over the rainbow.

MORE ART FUN!

☆ Collect scraps of fabric and sort them according to color, such as red, orange, yellow, green, blue, and violet. Draw arcs of a rainbow onto an old white sheet. Glue fabric onto the rainbow, using a separate color in each arc and overlapping the fabric's edges.

☆ Have you ever seen a rainbow after a rain shower? The colors in the rainbow are always in the exact same order: red, orange, yellow, green, blue, indigo (a shade of blue), and violet.

☆ Read The Rainbow Goblins by Ul De Rico.

Flower Garden

*Flowers come in many colors
that may not all suit you,
Go ahead and please yourself,
paint them black or blue!*

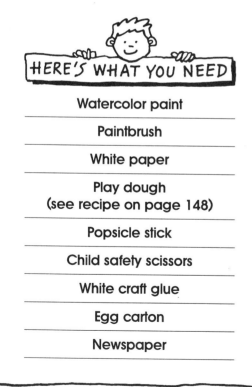

HERE'S WHAT YOU NEED

Watercolor paint

Paintbrush

White paper

Play dough
(see recipe on page 148)

Popsicle stick

Child safety scissors

White craft glue

Egg carton

Newspaper

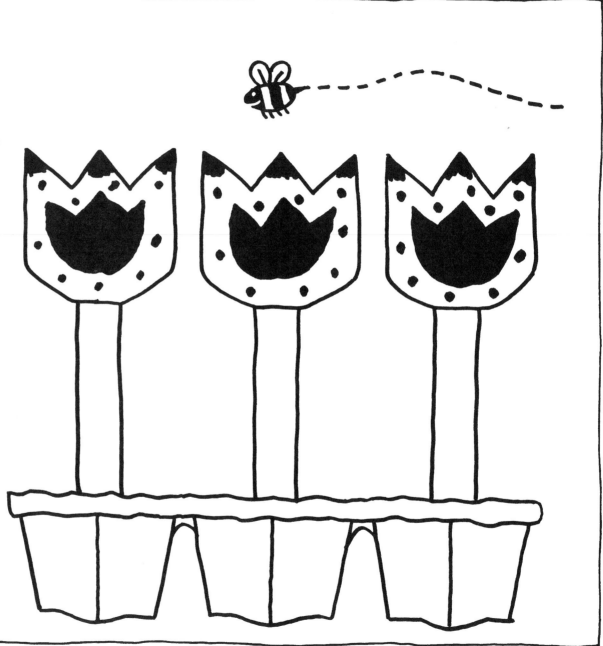

HERE'S WHAT YOU DO

1 Cover table with newspaper.

2 Use scissors to cut out heads of flowers from white paper. Paint the flowers with watercolor paint. Allow to dry completely.

3 Glue flowers onto Popsicle sticks for stems. Pour a small drop of glue into each egg carton compartment. Press play dough into glue; then allow to dry completely.

4 Poke Popsicle stick flowers into play dough for a garden.

MORE ART FUN!

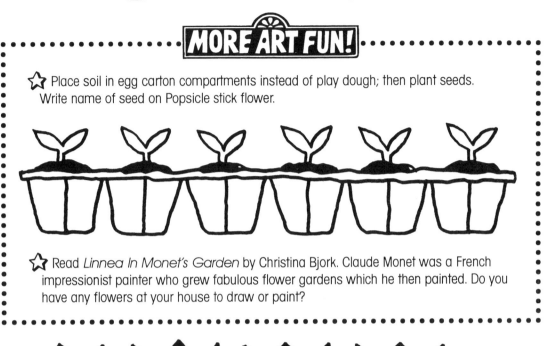

☆ Place soil in egg carton compartments instead of play dough; then plant seeds. Write name of seed on Popsicle stick flower.

☆ Read *Linnea In Monet's Garden* by Christina Bjork. Claude Monet was a French impressionist painter who grew fabulous flower gardens which he then painted. Do you have any flowers at your house to draw or paint?

CUT OUT FLOWER HEADS

WHITE PAPER

GLUE FLOWER HEAD TO STICK

DECORATE FLOWER HEADS

PAINT STICK STEMS GREEN

PUSH IN STEMS

PLAY DOUGH

GLUE

Paper Bag Pet

*If your pets need pizazz,
because they look too plain,
Paint tiger stripes and leopard spots
and hope it doesn't rain!*

HERE'S WHAT YOU NEED

Poster paint

Paintbrush

Container of water

Two small brown paper bags

String

Newspaper

Tape

HERE'S WHAT YOU DO

1 Cover table with newspaper.

2 Use poster paint to paint stripes or spots on one paper bag and allow to dry completely.

3 Stuff second paper bag with newspaper. Tape top of the bag closed.

4 Slip painted bag over top of stuffed bag to keep animal upright.

5 Tie string around bags to make animal's neck.

DECORATE ONE BAG

STUFF THE OTHER BAG

PUT PAINTED BAG OVER STUFFED BAG AND TIE WITH STRING FOR NECK

MORE ART FUN!

☆ Use safety scissors to cut eyes, ears, mouth, and tail from construction paper; then glue them onto paper bag pet.

← EARS- MAKE 2

TAIL-MAKE!

EYES-MAKE 2

☆ If you have a cat at your house, then you know one member of the cat family, but there are quite a few others. Can you name them? What about lions, tigers, the bobcat, and the lynx? What would you add to a cat drawing to make it look like a lion or tiger?

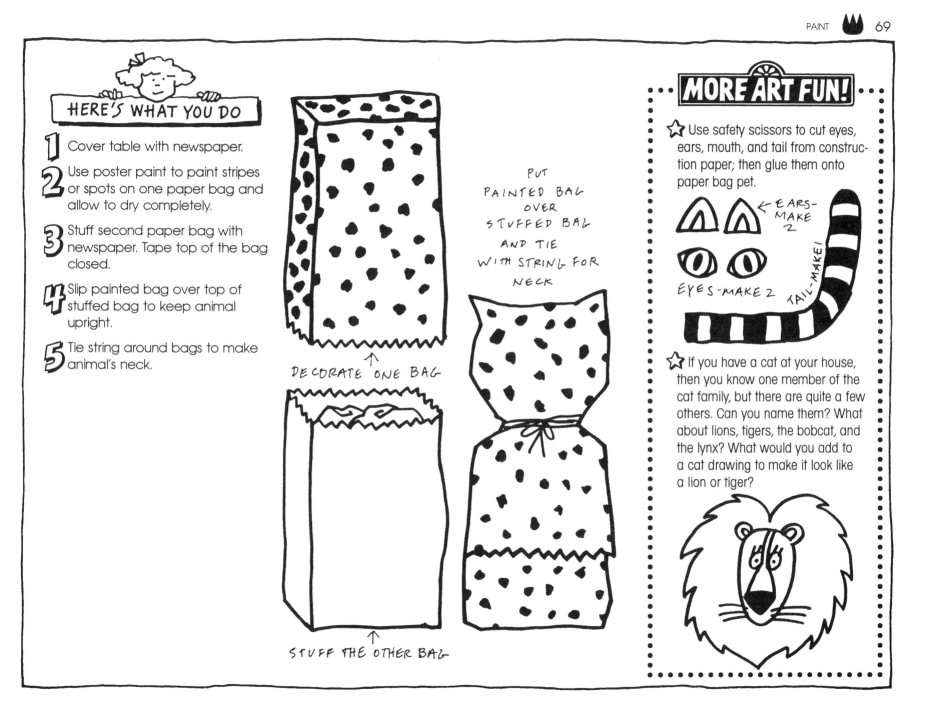

Vegetable Prints

*When dinner is served,
and there's onions, corn, and beets,
Make vegetable prints,
and find something else to eat!*

HERE'S WHAT YOU NEED

Poster paint

**Raw vegetables
(such as onions, carrots, corn-on-the-cob, celery, and potatoes)**

***Sharp knife
(for grown-up use only)**

Heavy paper plate

Sheet of paper

Newspaper

CUT

MUSHROOMS

ORANGES

POTATOES

BROCCOLI

HERE'S WHAT YOU DO

1. Cover table with newspaper.

2. Ask a grown-up to use the knife to cut vegetables with a flat surface showing.

3. Pour a thin layer of paint into a heavy paper plate. Dip the flat side of vegetables in paint. Press vegetables onto paper for vegetable prints.

MORE ART FUN!

☆ Use things such as a plastic berry basket, cork, potato masher, and other gadgets to dip into paint for a print.

☆ Do you have a vegetable garden? No matter where you live – even if you have a small stoop or sunny windowsill – you can grow a cherry tomato plant. You need a medium-sized clay pot, some potting soil, a healthy plant, and some water. Plant your plant, water it, place in a sunny spot, and watch it grow. Yum!

Painted Rocks

*Paint colors of the ocean
on pebbles from the shore,
Every time you look at them,
you'll see the ocean floor!*

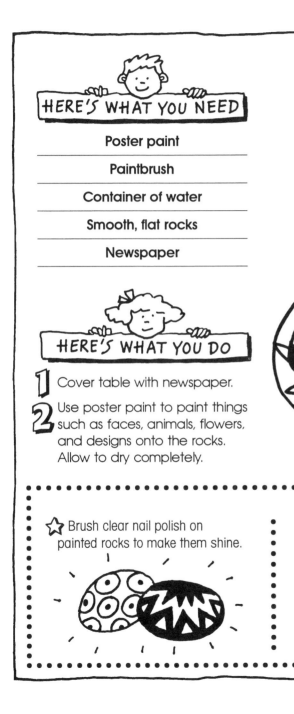

HERE'S WHAT YOU NEED

Poster paint

Paintbrush

Container of water

Smooth, flat rocks

Newspaper

HERE'S WHAT YOU DO

1 Cover table with newspaper.

2 Use poster paint to paint things such as faces, animals, flowers, and designs onto the rocks. Allow to dry completely.

MORE ART FUN!

☆ Brush clear nail polish on painted rocks to make them shine.

☆ Glue things such as yarn, pipe cleaners, and dried beans onto painted rocks for hair, whiskers, and eyes of faces and animals.

☆ Start a small rock collection. Look for rocks with unusual shapes, unusual colors, rocks that fit in your hand perfectly, rocks that are very smooth, and rocks that sparkle. Sort them into piles (all smooth rocks together, for example) and keep in egg carton compartments.

Paper Bag Pumpkin

*Paint a Halloween picture
and wait until it's dry,
Add a jack-o'-lantern's face
and eat some pumpkin pie!*

HERE'S WHAT YOU NEED

Poster paint (orange)

Paintbrush

Brown paper lunch bag

Construction paper (black)

Child safety scissors

White craft glue

Rubber band

Newspaper

HERE'S WHAT YOU DO

1. Cover table with newspaper.

2. Fill paper bag with crumpled newspaper. Tightly wrap the rubber band around neck of bag for pumpkin's stem.

3. Paint stuffed bag with orange poster paint and allow to dry completely.

4. Meanwhile, use scissors to cut out the jack-o-lantern's eyes, nose, and mouth from black construction paper. Glue them onto the paper bag pumpkin.

MORE ART FUN!

☆ Use scissors to cut a stem from green construction paper; then glue stem into top of pumpkin. Make additional paper bag pumpkins for a pumpkin patch.

☆ Read *Popcorn* by Frank Asch for an unusual twist on Halloween.

STUFF BAG WITH PAPER

WRAP RUBBER BAND AROUND BAG

CUT OUT EYES, NOSE, AND MOUTH THEN GLUE THEM ON BAG

PAINT BAG ORANGE

Valentine Mobile

*A mobile is a sculpture
with many moving parts.
Make one for your Valentine
by hanging up some hearts!*

HERE'S WHAT YOU NEED

Poster paint (red and white)

Paintbrush

Container of water

Construction paper

Wire clothes hanger

Child safety scissors

String

Newspaper

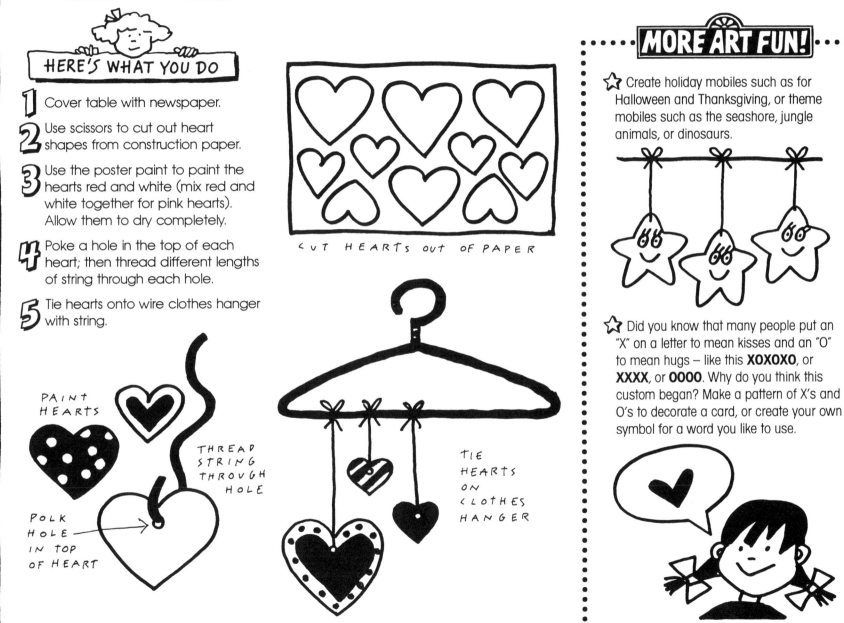

HERE'S WHAT YOU DO

1. Cover table with newspaper.

2. Use scissors to cut out heart shapes from construction paper.

3. Use the poster paint to paint the hearts red and white (mix red and white together for pink hearts). Allow them to dry completely.

4. Poke a hole in the top of each heart; then thread different lengths of string through each hole.

5. Tie hearts onto wire clothes hanger with string.

CUT HEARTS OUT OF PAPER

PAINT HEARTS

THREAD STRING THROUGH HOLE

POLK HOLE IN TOP OF HEART

TIE HEARTS ON CLOTHES HANGER

MORE ART FUN!

☆ Create holiday mobiles such as for Halloween and Thanksgiving, or theme mobiles such as the seashore, jungle animals, or dinosaurs.

☆ Did you know that many people put an "X" on a letter to mean kisses and an "O" to mean hugs — like this **XOXOXO**, or **XXXX**, or **OOOO**. Why do you think this custom began? Make a pattern of X's and O's to decorate a card, or create your own symbol for a word you like to use.

Clothespin Butterfly

*Butterfly wings of paper
will flutter in the breeze,
Just gather in the center,
and give a little squeeze!*

HERE'S WHAT YOU NEED

Watercolor paints

Paintbrush

Container of water

White tissue paper or
paper towel

Spring-type clothespin

Pipe cleaner

DECORATE PAPER
WITH WATERCOLORS

FOLD PAPER BACK AND FORTH

1 Paint with watercolors on tissue paper or paper towel; then allow to dry completely.

2 Fold paper accordion-style back and forth onto itself like a fan. Pinch paper in center with clothespin for butterfly.

3 Wrap pipe cleaner around head of clothespin for butterfly's antennae.

MORE ART FUN!

☆ Use scissors to cut shape of a butterfly from white paper plate. Paint butterfly with watercolor paint; then allow to dry completely. Use markers to add things such as markings on butterfly's wings.

☆ Butterflies are so beautiful to look at as they flutter around and land on flowers. Don't touch — just look and admire. Then think of all the things in the world that fly. **How many** can you name?

PINCH PAPER IN CENTER WITH CLOTHESPIN

WRAP PIPE CLEANER AROUND HEAD

Dancing Fingers

*If listening to music,
makes you tap your feet,
Fingers dipped in finger paint,
will wiggle to the beat!*

HERE'S WHAT YOU NEED

**Finger paint
(see recipe on page 150)**

Glossy white paper (shelf paper)

Container of water

Popsicle stick or spoon

**Radio, tape player, or other
source of music**

Newspaper

HERE'S WHAT YOU DO

1 Cover table with newspaper.

2 Sprinkle a few drops of water to dampen glossy paper. Use Popsicle stick to scoop a small glob of finger paint onto paper.

3 Listen to music while using fingers to spread finger paint around paper.

MORE ART FUN!

☆ Allow finger painting to dry completely. Use painting for wrapping gifts or to cover a book.

☆ Run a plastic comb across finger paint for a design.

☆ Place a thin sheet of paper on top of wet finger painting. Rub hand lightly back and forth over paper; then lift for print of finger painting.

Light & Dark

Mixing black with colors can turn them dark as night, For colors bright as sunshine, try mixing them with white!

HERE'S WHAT YOU NEED

Poster paint
(red, yellow, blue, white, and black)

Construction paper in
black and white

Paintbrush

Container of water

Muffin tin

Popsicle sticks

HERE'S WHAT YOU DO

1 Pour each color of paint into two compartments of muffin tin. Add a drop of black paint to color in one compartment; add a drop of white paint to same color in other compartment. Do this until all colors have a drop of white or black paint added to them for light and dark shades of the same color.

2 Use Popsicle sticks to mix each color.

3 Paint colors onto black and white construction paper for contrasting pictures.

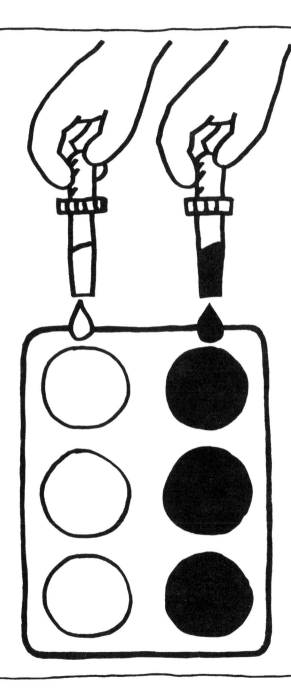

MORE ART FUN!

☆ Paint with dark colors for a rainy day picture; use light colors for a sunny day picture.

☆ Talk about how you feel when the sun is shining and how you feel on rainy days.

☆ Talk about which colors you like best – bright or dark.

Dripping Colors

If raindrops fell from clouds
in red, yellow, and blue,
You could dip into a puddle
for colors that are new!

FOLD PAPER INTO EIGHTHS

DIP CORNERS
OF FOLDED
PAPER INTO
COLORS

HERE'S WHAT YOU NEED

Food coloring

White paper towel

Muffin tin

Water

HERE'S WHAT YOU DO

1 Add ¼ cup (50 ml) water (reduce for more intense color) to each muffin tin compartment. Add food coloring (mix colors together for new colors) to water in each compartment.

2 Fold paper towel into eighths or sixteenths.

3 Dip one corner of folded towel into one color; then dip another corner into another color. Continue dipping the corners of the towel until many colors have been absorbed.

4 Unfold towel and allow to dry completely.

MORE ART FUN!

☆ Use scissors to cut a snowflake design in the folded towel before dipping it into colors.

☆ Use an eye dropper to drip food color onto the towel.

☆ Dip absorbent papers such as coffee filters, white tissue paper, or wet typing paper into colors.

Roller Painting

*If you're tired of a paintbrush,
try something that is new,
Dip a roller into paint,
it's fast and easy too!*

HERE'S WHAT YOU NEED

Poster paint

Large sheet of paper

Paint roller

Baking pan

HERE'S WHAT YOU DO

1 Pour poster paint into baking pan.

2 Roll the roller back and forth in the paint; then paint with roller on large sheet of paper.

3 Add additional colors of paint to baking pan, and then roll over-lapping colors onto paper.

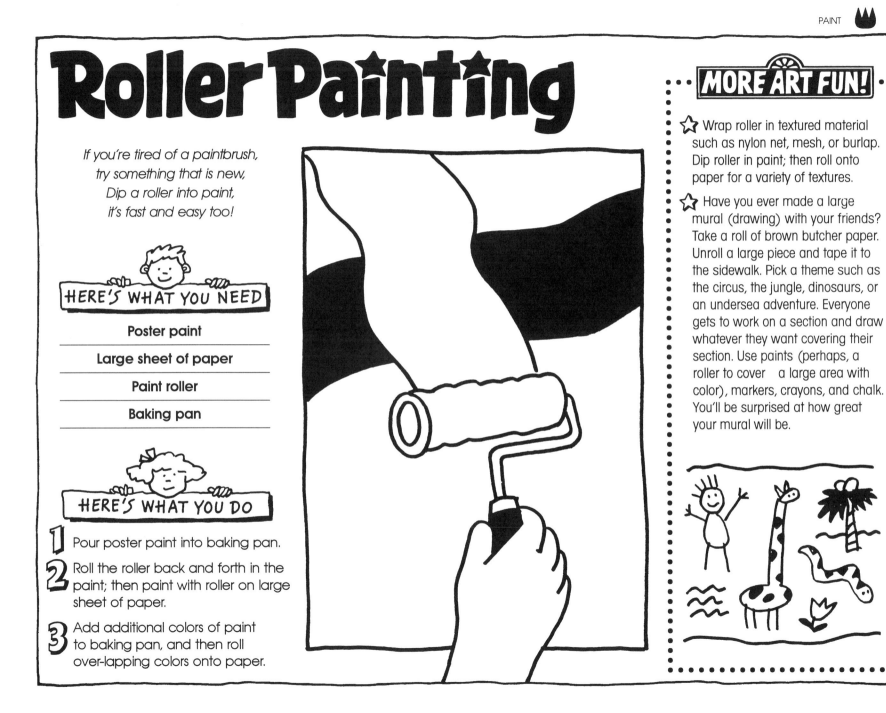

MORE ART FUN!

☆ Wrap roller in textured material such as nylon net, mesh, or burlap. Dip roller in paint; then roll onto paper for a variety of textures.

☆ Have you ever made a large mural (drawing) with your friends? Take a roll of brown butcher paper. Unroll a large piece and tape it to the sidewalk. Pick a theme such as the circus, the jungle, dinosaurs, or an undersea adventure. Everyone gets to work on a section and draw whatever they want covering their section. Use paints (perhaps, a roller to cover a large area with color), markers, crayons, and chalk. You'll be surprised at how great your mural will be.

Alphabet Stencil

*Letters of the alphabet
spell words that may be new,
They start with A for apple,
and end with Z for zoo!*

Poster paint (bright color)

Paper plate

Two sheets of white paper

Sponge

Child safety scissors

Tape

HERE'S WHAT YOU DO

1 Use scissors to cut letters into center of one sheet of paper.

2 Lay paper with cut out letters over second sheet of paper. Tape two sheets together.

3 Pour small amount of paint onto paper plate. Dip corner of sponge into paint.

4 Dab sponge over letters until it is covered with paint; then lift off top sheet of paper to see letters.

5 Repeat the process, moving the stencil around the paper.

MORE ART FUN!

☆ Fold construction paper into fourths for personalized stationery. Stencil front of the card with your initials; then open card and write a greeting inside.

☆ Use scissors to cut out other shapes of stencils such as numbers, hearts, and flowers.

CLAY & DOUGH

You can pinch and squeeze and roll,
a little ball of clay,
It goes the way you want it to,
then knows just how to stay!

Tiny Trees

*So you want to climb a tree —
and need one that's very small,
Find a twig to plant in clay
'cause it won't grow at all!*

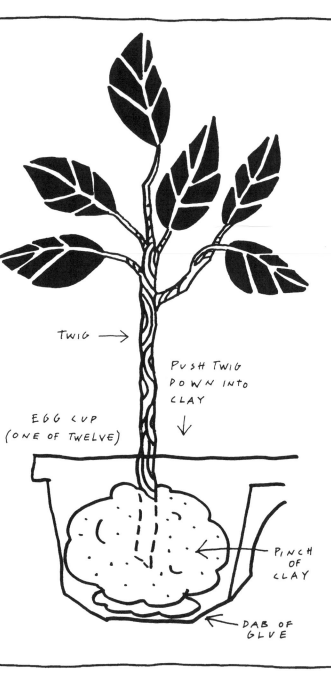

TWIG →

PUSH TWIG
DOWN INTO
CLAY
↓

EGG CUP
(ONE OF TWELVE)

PINCH
OF
CLAY
←

DAB OF
GLUE ←

HERE'S WHAT YOU NEED

**Salt clay or play dough
(see recipe on page 148)**

Egg carton

Twelve twigs

White craft glue

HERE'S WHAT YOU DO

1. Pinch off twelve pieces of clay.

2. Pour a small drop of glue into each egg compartment.

3. Press one piece of clay into each compartment and allow it to dry completely.

4. Poke one twig into clay in each compartment for a forest of small trees.

MORE ART FUN!

☆ Use scissors to cut small leaves from tissue paper; then glue leaves onto twigs.

☆ Pull apart a cotton ball; then glue strands of cotton onto twigs for snow.

☆ Gather some leaves on an autumn day. Bring them home and sort them by **color**: reds in one pile, yellows in another, browns in another, and greens in another. Which pile has the most leaves? Which pile has the **fewest** leaves? Now paste them on some paper and hang them on your bedroom door.

Clay Bird's Nest

*If a feathered friend needs a home,
build it a nest from clay,
Then make it cozy and warm
with soft grass and some hay!*

HERE'S WHAT YOU NEED

**Salt clay
(see recipe on page 148)**

Small, heavy-duty paper plate

Dried plant material

HERE'S WHAT YOU DO

1 Shape a large ball of clay to resemble a bird's nest.

2 Shape a small ball of clay to resemble a bird.

3 Place nest and bird onto paper plate and allow to dry completely.

4 Cushion nest with dried plant materials such as leaves, grass, and straw. Place bird into the nest.

MORE ART FUN!

☆ Poke feathers into clay bird; then allow to dry completely. Paint bird with poster paint.

☆ Shape bird's eggs from a ball of clay. Allow them to dry, paint them, and then place them into nest.

☆ Have you ever seen a robin's egg? It is such a beautiful bright blue that some people call it robin's egg blue. What are your favorite colors? Can you give them a name from nature like daffodil yellow or cardinal red?

Clay Porcupine

*Instead of cooking pasta,
here's a recipe for you,
Stick the pasta in a ball of clay
and make porcupine stew!*

HERE'S WHAT YOU DO

1 Shape ball of clay to resemble the body of a porcupine.

2 Break the spaghetti into pieces and poke them into the clay body.

3 Break Popsicle sticks in half; then push them into the clay body for porcupine's legs (the porcupine should stand upright). Allow it to dry completely.

MORE ART FUN!

☆ Create different clay animals by pressing pasta such as penne, elbow macaroni, or fuscilli into clay. Try making a dinosaur, armadillo, or alligator.

☆ Porcupines use their sharp quills to protect themselves from other animals. Can you think of ways other animals protect themselves?

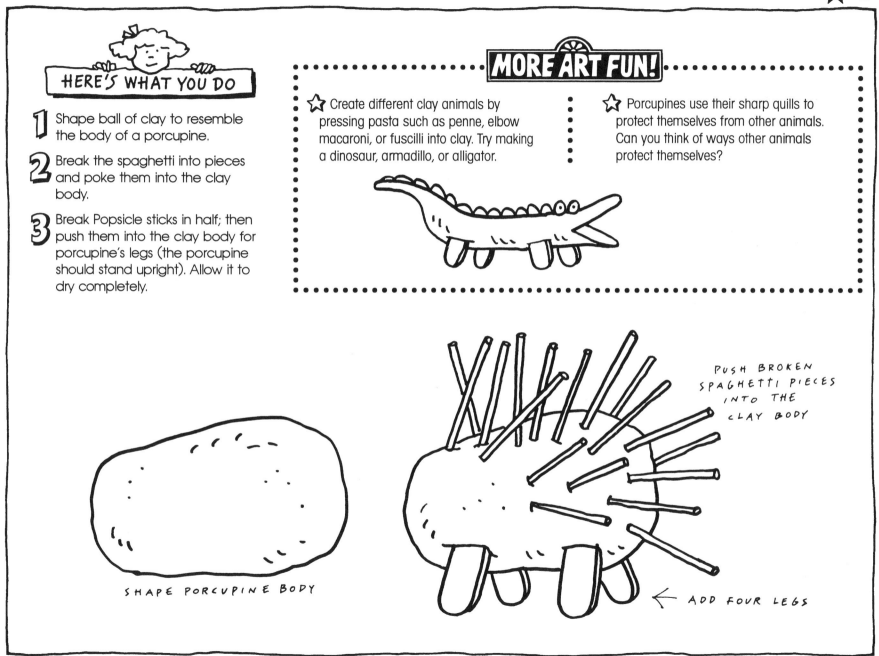

PUSH BROKEN SPAGHETTI PIECES INTO THE CLAY BODY

SHAPE PORCUPINE BODY

← ADD FOUR LEGS

Clay Octopus

Give an octopus extra arms
when it's made from clay,
Put it on your baseball team and
see how well it plays!

HERE'S WHAT YOU NEED

Salt clay
(see recipe on page 148)

Paper plate

Poster paint

Paintbrush

HERE'S WHAT YOU DO

1. Divide the clay in half. Shape one half into a ball for the octopus's body.

2. Pinch off eight pieces of clay from other half. Place each piece of clay between palms of hands. Rotate hands back and forth until a rope forms for each of the octopus's legs.

3. Firmly pinch each leg to the octopus's body.

4. Place octopus on a paper plate and allow to dry completely.

5. Paint octopus with poster paint.

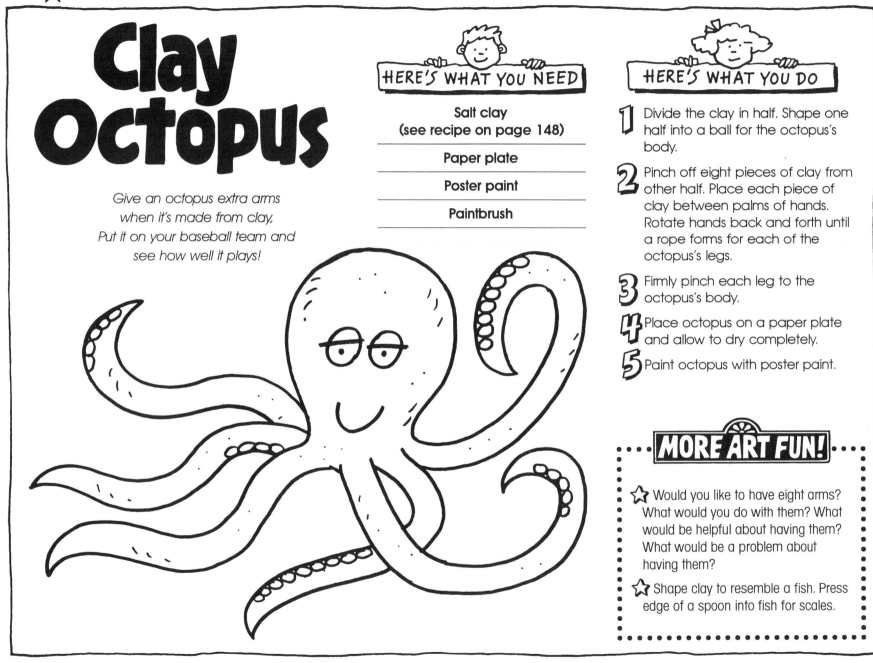

MORE ART FUN!

☆ Would you like to have eight arms? What would you do with them? What would be helpful about having them? What would be a problem about having them?

☆ Shape clay to resemble a fish. Press edge of a spoon into fish for scales.

Pinch Pot

*Put your thumb in a ball of clay
then pinch and squeeze a lot,
Go 'round and 'round and soon you'll see,
it turns into a pot!*

HERE'S WHAT YOU NEED

Salt clay
(see recipe on page 148)

Poster paint

Paintbrush

HERE'S WHAT YOU DO

1 Roll the clay into a ball.

2 Poke a thumb into center of ball to form an opening.

3 Pinch the opening wider while turning ball to form a pot. Allow to dry completely.

4 Paint the pot with poster paint.

MORE ART FUN!

☆ Press things such as tines of a fork or the tip of a spoon against the clay pot for texture.

☆ Brush on clear nail polish for painted pot to shine.

☆ Visit a craft center or potter's studio. Watch how potter's use a potter's wheel, how they keep the clay wet, and how they shape their pots. Ask about applying color with glazes. How hot does the kiln get? Would you like to be a potter someday?

Handprint Paperweight

Spread your fingers open wide,
Then press them into clay,
What a pretty print they make,
When you take your hand away!

HERE'S WHAT YOU NEED

Salt clay
(see recipe on page 148)

Rolling pin

Plastic knife

Poster paint

Paintbrush

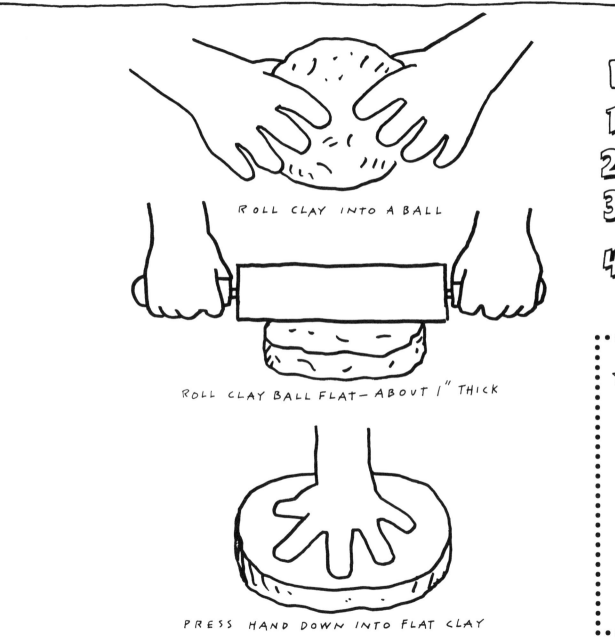

ROLL CLAY INTO A BALL

ROLL CLAY BALL FLAT—ABOUT 1" THICK

PRESS HAND DOWN INTO FLAT CLAY

HERE'S WHAT YOU DO

1 Use the rolling pin to flatten ball of clay to one inch (2.5 cm) thickness.

2 Press hand firmly into the clay for a handprint.

3 Use the plastic knife to trim edges of handprint. Allow to dry completely.

4 Paint handprint paperweight with poster paint.

MORE ART FUN!

☆ Use a pointed tool to write the name and date of the handprint in the clay. Allow it to dry completely; then paint it with poster paint.

MY HAND · JULY 1

Clay Cookies

To make a batch of cookies,
use a rolling pin,
Pretend your clay is cookie dough,
then let the fun begin!

HERE'S WHAT YOU NEED

Salt clay
(see recipe on page 148)

Rolling pin

Paper plate

Cookie cutters

HERE'S WHAT YOU DO

1 Use rolling pin to flatten the ball of clay.

2 Use cookie cutters to cut shapes from the dough.

3 Place the clay cookies on the paper plate. Allow them to dry completely.

MORE ART FUN!

☆ Press dried beans into clay cookies for pretend raisins.

☆ Shape the salt clay dough into letters or numbers. Allow to dry completely; then paint with poster paint.

☆ Ask a grown-up to help you bake some real, edible cookies. Does the real cookie dough feel different from the clay? Is it **more sticky** or **less sticky**? What are other **differences**? In what ways are the two doughs the same?

Meatballs & Spaghetti

*It's simple to make meatballs
if you roll them out of clay,
Just put them on spaghetti,
and serve them up that way!*

HERE'S WHAT YOU NEED

Salt clay
(see recipe on page 148)

Styrofoam tray
(from fruits and vegetables)

Poster paint

Paintbrush

HERE'S WHAT YOU DO

1. Place a piece of clay between palms of hands and rotate hands counterclockwise until a meatball forms. Place a piece of clay between palms of hands and rotate hands back and forth until spaghetti forms. Use palm of hand to flatten a ball of clay, then turn up edges for a plate.

2. Place clay plate on heavy-duty paper plate. Then, put the spaghetti and meatballs on your clay plate. Allow them to dry completely.

3. Paint plate of meatballs and spaghetti with poster paint.

MORE ART FUN!

☆ Shape foods such as a hot dog, pizza, and grapes from salt clay. Allow to dry completely; then paint with poster paint.

☆ If you were planning a special birthday dinner, what would you eat? Cut out pictures of your favorite foods from old magazines. Glue pictures on a piece of paper and hang on your refrigerator door.

Clay Snowman

*Build a snowman that won't melt
from three sizes of clay balls,
They sit atop each other,
the head's the one that's small!*

HERE'S WHAT YOU NEED

**Salt clay
(see recipe on page 148)**

Toothpicks

White craft glue

Dried beans

Piece of cardboard

HERE'S WHAT YOU DO

1 Shape clay into three balls: small, medium, and large.

2 Stick a toothpick halfway into the largest ball. Press the medium-sized ball onto the toothpick. Stick another toothpick into the medium ball. Press the smallest ball onto that toothpick for head of snowman (break toothpicks in half if they're too long).

3 Squeeze a drop of glue onto beans; then press them into snowman for eyes, nose, and mouth. Place snowman on piece of cardboard. Allow it to dry completely.

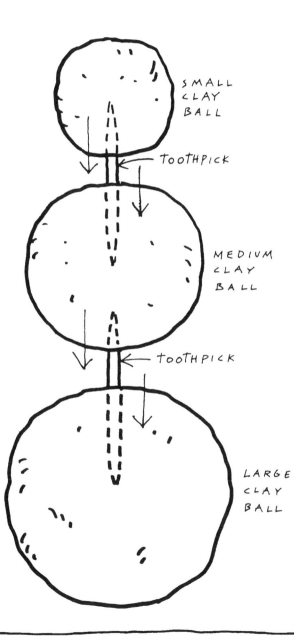

SMALL CLAY BALL

TOOTHPICK

MEDIUM CLAY BALL

TOOTHPICK

LARGE CLAY BALL

MORE ART FUN!

☆ Poke pipe cleaners into snowman for arms. Tie a small scrap of fabric around neck for snowman's scarf.

☆ **Small**, **medium**, and **large** are funny words because something can actually be small and medium and large, too. You are large compared to your baby brother or sister, but you are small compared to your mom or dad. Isn't that strange? What other things are small and medium and large?

Clay Beads

*Little balls of clay
become a necklace or a ring,
With a hole poked in the middle,
and a special piece of string!*

HERE'S WHAT YOU NEED

Salt clay
(see recipe on page 148)

Nail

Yarn

Pipe cleaner

Poster paint

Paintbrush

HERE'S WHAT YOU DO

1 Place small pieces of clay between palms of hands. Rotate hands counterclockwise until a ball forms for the beads. Make additional beads for necklace.

2 Push nail into centers of beads and wiggle it around to widen the hole.

3 Allow the beads to dry completely, making sure holes stay open. Paint the beads with poster paint.

4 Twist tip of pipe cleaner to form a small loop. Thread yarn through the loop as if it were a needle. Tie a thick knot in end of yarn.

5 Use the pipe cleaner to string the beads onto the yarn for a necklace.

MORE ART FUN!

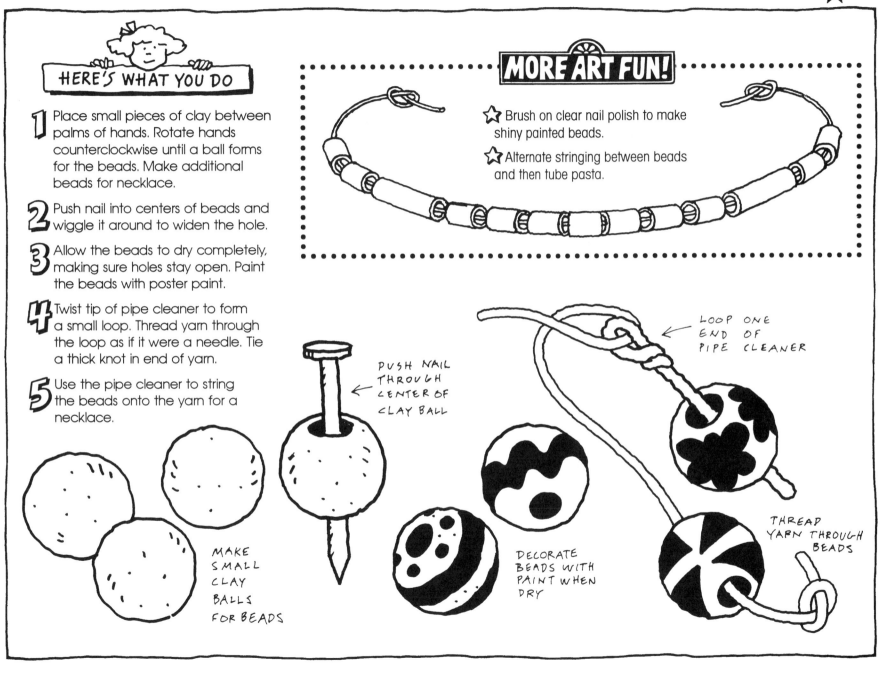

☆ Brush on clear nail polish to make shiny painted beads.

☆ Alternate stringing between beads and then tube pasta.

PUSH NAIL THROUGH CENTER OF CLAY BALL

LOOP ONE END OF PIPE CLEANER

MAKE SMALL CLAY BALLS FOR BEADS

DECORATE BEADS WITH PAINT WHEN DRY

THREAD YARN THROUGH BEADS

Clay Creatures

*Make silly creatures out of clay
that no one's seen before,
Give them necks and a tail,
then teach them how to roar!*

HERE'S WHAT YOU NEED

Salt clay
(see recipe on page 148)

Toothpicks

Pipe cleaner

Poster paint

Paintbrush

HERE'S WHAT YOU DO

1 Shape ball of clay into head and body of an animal.

2 Poke a toothpick halfway into the clay body. Press clay head onto this toothpick.

3 Poke pipe cleaner into your creature for a tail. Allow clay to dry completely.

4 Paint your creatures with poster paint.

MORE ART FUN!

☆ Turn a shoe box on its side and paint trees and leaves on the inside of box. Place creatures in box for a diorama.

☆ Read the story *Big Trouble* by Jacquie Hann to see just what can happen with a ball of clay!

MARKERS

*When your artwork needs some color
that is very clear and bright,
Use markers for your drawings,
And also when you write!*

Sewing Pictures

*Learn to thread a needle
and you'll never go bare,
'Cause you'll know how to sew
the clothes you want to wear!*

HERE'S WHAT YOU NEED

Markers

Shirt cardboard

Hole punch

Child safety scissors

Yarn

*Thick needle

HERE'S WHAT YOU DO

1 Use scissors to cut the shirt cardboard into shapes. Punch holes around edge of shape and as far into the center as possible.

2 Use the markers to draw on the cardboard shape.

3 Thread needle with the yarn.

4 Sew in and out of the holes with the needle and yarn for a sewing picture. You can remove yarn to use sewing cards again and again.

☆ To sew without a needle, dip end of yarn in white craft glue. Press yarn end together and let dry completely. Yarn end will be stiff enough to sew cards without a needle.

☆ Use safety scissors to cut out a picture from an old magazine. Glue it onto the cardboard; then punch holes around the picture. Sew in and out with needle and yarn.

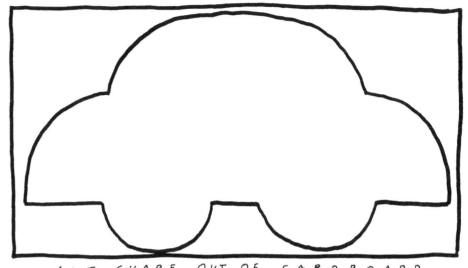

CUT SHAPE OUT OF CARDBOARD

SEW IN AND OUT OF HOLES

Spoon Puppet

*Draw a face with markers
on a spoon that's made of wood,
Glue on yarn for hair
to look like a puppet should!*

HERE'S WHAT YOU NEED

Markers

Wooden spoon

Poster paint
(white, brown, tan, yellow)

Paintbrush

White craft glue

Scrap fabric

Yarn

Newspapers

HERE'S WHAT YOU DO

1 Cover table with newspapers.

2 Paint the wooden spoon any skin tone, and allow to dry completely.

3 Use markers to draw a face on bowl of the spoon.

4 Glue yarn onto back and top of the bowl for the puppet's hair.

5 Glue scrap fabric onto handle of the spoon for the puppet's costume.

PAINT WOODEN SPOON

DRAW FACE

GLUE ON YARN HAIR

GLUE FABRIC ON HANDLE

MORE ART FUN!

☆ Use markers to draw a face on a small paper plate. Glue on yarn for hair; then glue the plate onto a Popsicle stick for a puppet.

☆ Cover a glass jar with a cone-shaped piece of construction paper (smaller at neck, wider at hem). Add pipe cleaner arms, fabric apron, and a paper flower in "hand." Prop spoon head inside jar. Give your Kitchen Doll to someone special for Mother's Day, Grandmother's Day, or any day for a happy surprise.

Sparkling Crowns

*Kings might use markers
to color gems ruby red,
They'd glue them in the crown
that rests atop their head!*

HERE'S WHAT YOU NEED

Markers

Recycled aluminum foil

Construction paper

Child safety scissors

White craft glue

Tape

HERE'S WHAT YOU DO

1 Use scissors to cut a band of construction paper 18 inches wide (46 cm). Measure the length to fit around head; then, cut a zigzag shape into top of the band.

2 Use markers to color the crown.

3 Cut pieces of foil in gem shapes and glue them onto the crown for jewels.

4 Overlap the ends and tape together.

CUT ZIGZAG-SHAPED BAND

DECORATE CROWN WITH MARKERS

MORE ART FUN!

☆ Glue things such as beads, cotton balls, and sequins onto base of the crown.

☆ Use scissors to cut sponges into shapes. Dip them into poster paint and press onto the crown for a print. Allow to dry completely.

☆ Talk about why you think the custom of kings and queens wearing crowns began.

☆ Make a crown of dandelions or daisies by braiding or weaving them together.

Colorful Kites

With paper and lots of string,
you can build a kite,
Color it with markers,
and it will look just right!

HERE'S WHAT YOU NEED

Markers

Paper bag (long and slender)

Florist's wire

String

Child safety scissors

Tape

HERE'S WHAT YOU DO

1. Use scissors to cut a small round hole in the bottom of the paper bag. Decorate the bag (kite) with brightly colored markers.

2. Form florist's wire into a circle larger than hole in the bag. Tape ends of the wire together.

3. Attach three bridle strings to the wire circle; then tie them together in a knot.

4. Put wire loop into sack. Pull the bridle string out through the hole in the bag for a kite.

5. Attach the kite-flying string to the bridle-string knot.

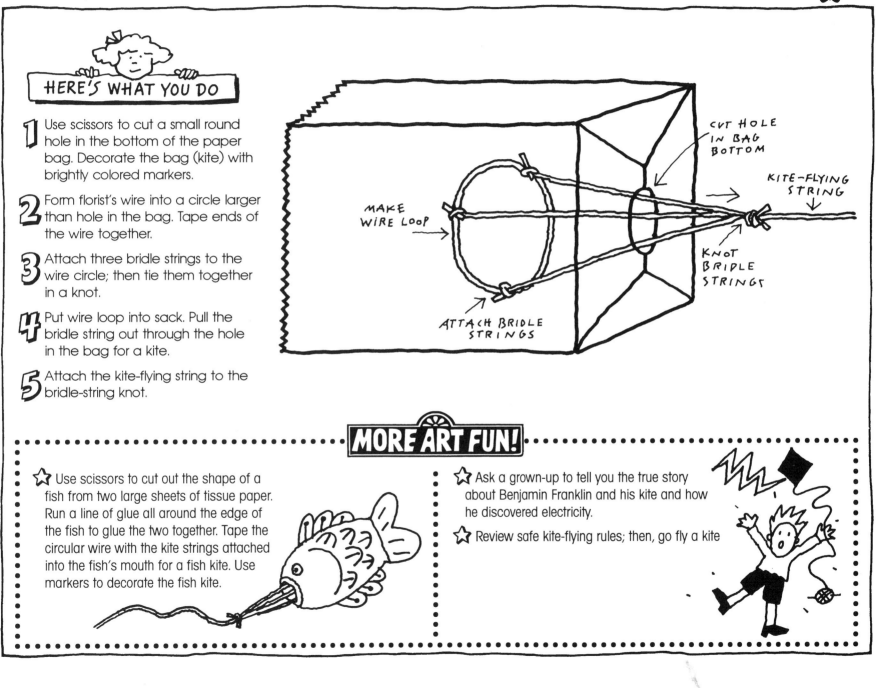

MAKE WIRE LOOP

ATTACH BRIDLE STRINGS

CUT HOLE IN BAG BOTTOM

KITE-FLYING STRING

KNOT BRIDLE STRINGS

MORE ART FUN!

☆ Use scissors to cut out the shape of a fish from two large sheets of tissue paper. Run a line of glue all around the edge of the fish to glue the two together. Tape the circular wire with the kite strings attached into the fish's mouth for a fish kite. Use markers to decorate the fish kite.

☆ Ask a grown-up to tell you the true story about Benjamin Franklin and his kite and how he discovered electricity.

☆ Review safe kite-flying rules; then, go fly a kite

Picture Mail

Use markers to draw a picture,
then fold it end to end,
Put it inside an envelope
and mail it to a friend!

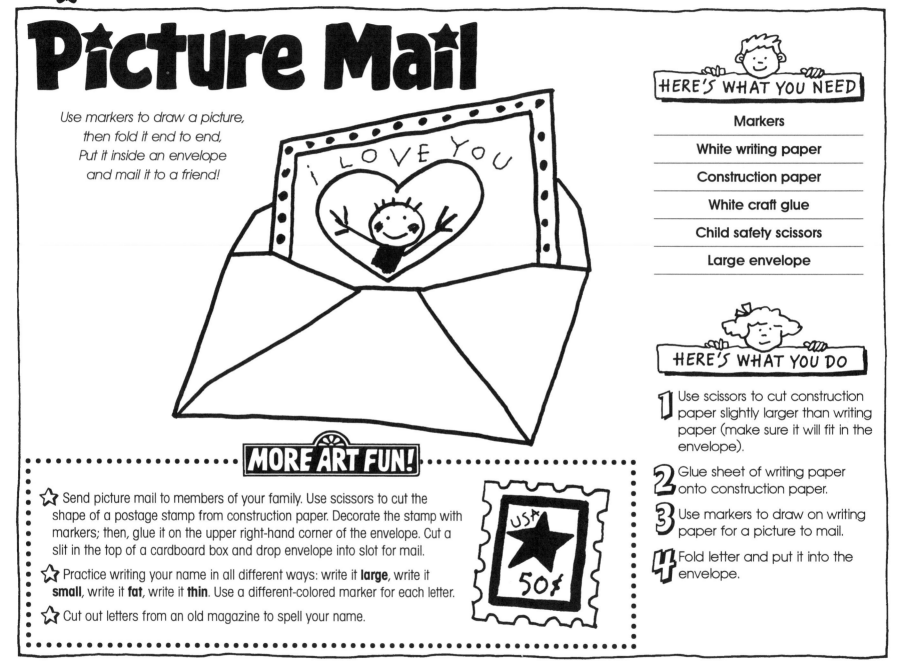

HERE'S WHAT YOU NEED

Markers

White writing paper

Construction paper

White craft glue

Child safety scissors

Large envelope

HERE'S WHAT YOU DO

1 Use scissors to cut construction paper slightly larger than writing paper (make sure it will fit in the envelope).

2 Glue sheet of writing paper onto construction paper.

3 Use markers to draw on writing paper for a picture to mail.

4 Fold letter and put it into the envelope.

MORE ART FUN!

☆ Send picture mail to members of your family. Use scissors to cut the shape of a postage stamp from construction paper. Decorate the stamp with markers; then, glue it on the upper right-hand corner of the envelope. Cut a slit in the top of a cardboard box and drop envelope into slot for mail.

☆ Practice writing your name in all different ways: write it **large**, write it **small**, write it **fat**, write it **thin**. Use a different-colored marker for each letter.

☆ Cut out letters from an old magazine to spell your name.

Bumpy Cardboard Rubbings

What's hiding under paper?
Well, you'll be glad to hear,
If you rub a marker,
soon it will appear!

HERE'S WHAT YOU NEED

Markers

Thin white paper

Shirt cardboard

Corrugated cardboard

Child safety scissors

White craft glue

HERE'S WHAT YOU DO

1. Expose the ridges of the corrugated cardboard by peeling back the thin paper covering. Use scissors to cut shapes from the cardboard.

2. Glue corrugated cardboard shapes onto shirt cardboard. Allow to dry.

3. Lay sheet of white paper on top of the shapes. Hold the paper in place while lightly rubbing the marker back and forth until texture and shape of corrugated cardboard appear.

MORE ART FUN!

☆ Paint corrugated cardboard shapes with poster paint. While still wet, lay a sheet of paper over the top. Rub lightly; then lift for a print.

☆ Take your markers and paper along with you for a walk in the woods. Hold paper up to a tree and gently rub markers (or crayons) over paper. You'll see the bark's pattern appear on your paper. Try this on different kinds of trees and compare the results. What do you notice? Are the bark rubbings all the **same**, or **different**?

Sun Catcher

*Draw with markers on plastic lids,
then when you are done,
Hang them in a window,
so they can catch the sun!*

HERE'S WHAT YOU NEED

Markers

**Clear plastic lids
from deli containers**

Hole punch

String

HERE'S WHAT YOU DO

1 Punch a hole in rim of plastic lid, then thread string through and tie with a knot.

2 Use markers to draw on the lid. Hang lid in a window to catch the sun.

PUT STRING THROUGH HOLE

PUNCH A HOLE IN THE LID

KNOT STRING

DRAW A PICTURE OR DESIGN ON LID

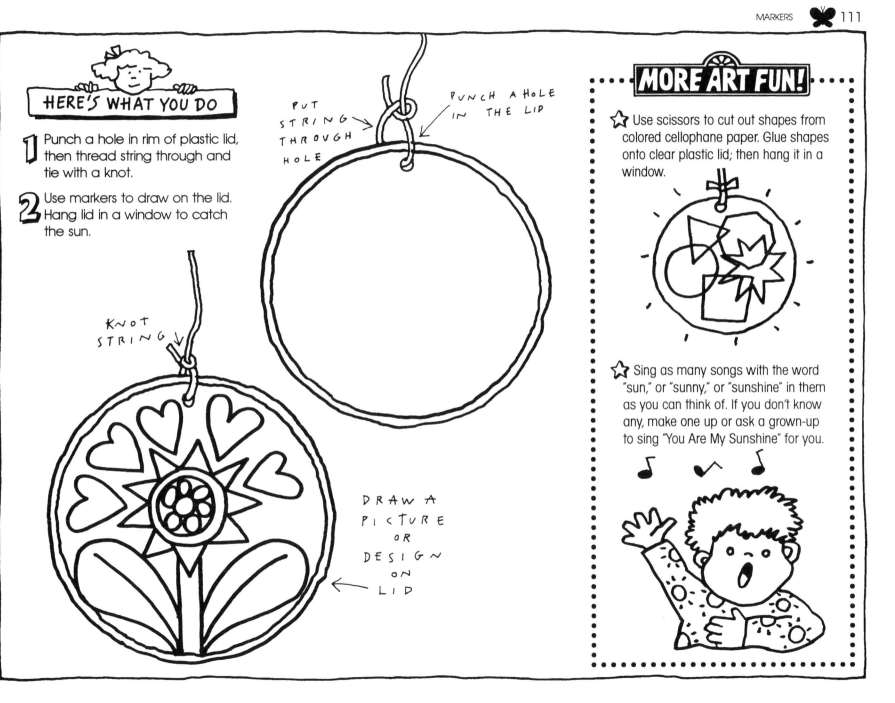

MORE ART FUN!

☆ Use scissors to cut out shapes from colored cellophane paper. Glue shapes onto clear plastic lid; then hang it in a window.

☆ Sing as many songs with the word "sun," or "sunny," or "sunshine" in them as you can think of. If you don't know any, make one up or ask a grown-up to sing "You Are My Sunshine" for you.

Triangle Stencils

*Use markers to draw a triangle
with a base that's very wide,
Make it pointy at the top,
then slope down the other side!*

HERE'S WHAT YOU NEED

Markers

Sheet of paper

**Styrofoam tray
(from fruits or vegetables)**

Child safety scissors

Pencil

HERE'S WHAT YOU DO

1. Use scissors to cut away rim of styrofoam tray.

2. Use pencil to draw the shape of a triangle in center of the tray. Cut out only the triangle, leaving a border of styrofoam around the shape.

3. Use markers to trace the triangle stencil onto sheet of paper.

4. Repeat triangle tracings, overlapping and moving them around the paper.

MORE ART FUN!

☆ Cut shapes such as circles and squares from the styrofoam tray. Use markers to trace the shapes onto paper. Staple sheets of paper together for a book of shapes.

☆ Take a walk down your street into town, or through your school. Look at the buildings, signs, benches, tables, windows, gardens, sidewalks. How many different places can you find triangles? circles? Draw some sketches of the triangles and circles around you.

CRAYONS

Open a box of crayons
and you will find inside,
Colors you've used before
and some you've never tried!

Crayon Resist

*If you color a picture with crayons,
and then get caught in the rain,
The paper will be soaking wet,
but the drawing will stay the same!*

HERE'S WHAT YOU NEED

Crayons

White paper

Watercolor paint

Paintbrush

Container of water

HERE'S WHAT YOU DO

1 Use crayons to color a picture on the white paper. Leave the background area uncolored.

2 Brush one color of paint over the entire drawing. The paint will stick only to the non-crayoned areas for a crayon resist drawing.

COLOR A PICTURE WITH CRAYONS ON WHITE PAPER

BRUSH PAINT OVER THE WHOLE PICTURE

BLUE

MORE ART FUN!

☆ Draw a picture with a white crayon on white paper; then brush watercolor paint over the paper for a magic picture to appear.

WHITE

☆ Crayon a design on hard-cooked eggs; then dip them in Easter egg dye or food color.

Crayon Fabric

When you draw on cotton,
the pattern's made by you,
Use many colors, and
your imagination, too!

HERE'S WHAT YOU NEED

Crayons

Cotton or muslin fabric

*Iron

Newspaper

HERE'S WHAT YOU DO

1 Ask a grown-up to set the iron on medium hot. Cover table with newspaper.

2 Use crayons to color a picture on a small piece of muslin or cotton (use old sheets). Press down hard on the crayon for a thick application.

3 Place fabric face down on a layer of newspaper; then cover it with a damp cloth. Place another layer of newspaper on top of the fabric.

4 Ask a grown-up to slide the iron back and forth over newspaper for a few seconds. Remove fabric when the crayons melt and colors are set into the cloth.

↓ N E W S P A P E R ↓

↓ D A M P   C L O T H ↓

↓ D R A W I N G   (FACE DOWN) ↓

↓ N E W S P A P E R ↓

MORE ART FUN!

☆ Use crayons to draw on cloth. Soak cloth in fabric dye or food color. Allow to dry completely. Then ask a grown-up to iron between sheets of newspaper for batik fabric.

☆ When you buy fabric in a fabric store you buy it "by the yard." (A yard is equal to 3 feet which is the same as 36 inches.) The fabric is stored in large bolts that are unrolled and cut to the size the customer needs. Visit a fabric store to see the different **colors**, **patterns**, and **textures** of fabric. Ask if they have any fabric scraps that you could have for your art projects.

Scratch Board

Cover a drawing with crayon,
until it's black as night,
Then scratch the surface and you'll see,
colors bold and bright!

HERE'S WHAT YOU NEED

Crayons (including black)

Shirt cardboard

**Toothpick, paper clip, or other
pointed object**

HERE'S WHAT YOU DO

1 Cover entire surface of shirt cardboard with bright crayon (younger children should work on a smaller piece of cardboard). Press down hard for rich, thick color.

2 Cover over the entire drawing with black crayon. Use a pointed object to scratch a design into black crayon surface to reveal bright colors underneath.

MORE ART FUN!

 Use scissors to cut out shapes such as a butterfly, flower, or fish from the cardboard. Use brightly colored crayons to color the shapes. Cover the colors with black crayon; then scratch the surface.

☆ Take some scrap paper and experiment with crayons. Press **lightly**; press **hard**. Color with one color over another. What happens when you **mix** yellow with blue? red with yellow? blue with red?

Melted Crayons

Heat will melt your crayons,
so remember on washing day,
Take them out of your pockets,
and put them all away!

HERE'S WHAT YOU NEED

Old crayons

Shiny white paper

Vegetable peeler

*Iron

Newspapers

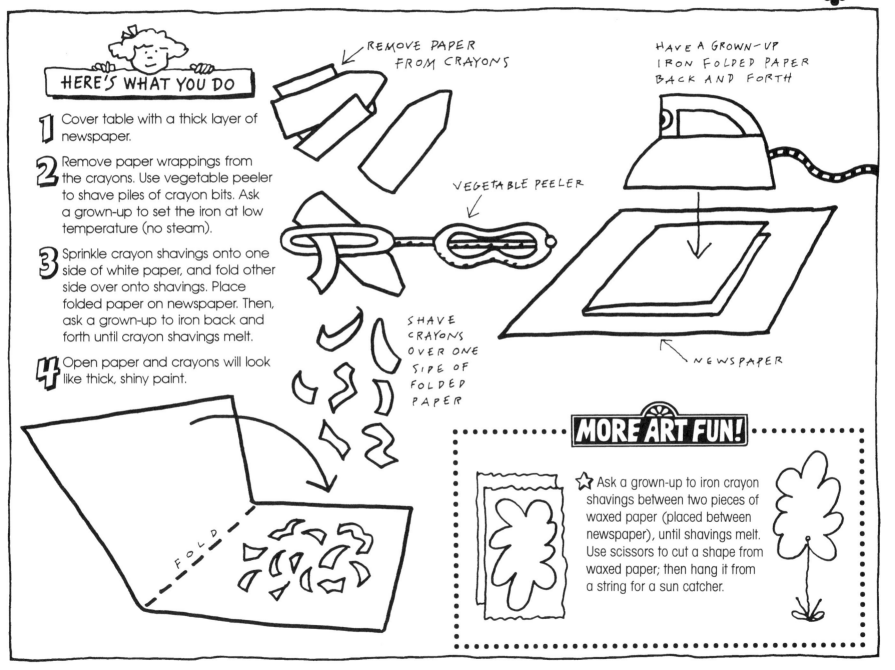

REMOVE PAPER
FROM CRAYONS

HAVE A GROWN-UP
IRON FOLDED PAPER
BACK AND FORTH

HERE'S WHAT YOU DO

1 Cover table with a thick layer of newspaper.

2 Remove paper wrappings from the crayons. Use vegetable peeler to shave piles of crayon bits. Ask a grown-up to set the iron at low temperature (no steam).

3 Sprinkle crayon shavings onto one side of white paper, and fold other side over onto shavings. Place folded paper on newspaper. Then, ask a grown-up to iron back and forth until crayon shavings melt.

4 Open paper and crayons will look like thick, shiny paint.

VEGETABLE PEELER

SHAVE
CRAYONS
OVER ONE
SIDE OF
FOLDED
PAPER

NEWSPAPER

FOLD

MORE ART FUN!

☆ Ask a grown-up to iron crayon shavings between two pieces of waxed paper (placed between newspaper), until shavings melt. Use scissors to cut a shape from waxed paper; then hang it from a string for a sun catcher.

Snowy Days

*If you're drawing a winter scene,
and lots of snow must fall,
Try using a white crayon or
glue on a cotton ball!*

HERE'S WHAT YOU NEED

White crayon

Construction paper
(dark colors, including blue)

Marker (black)

Child safety scissors

Cotton ball

White craft glue

HERE'S WHAT YOU DO

1 Use scissors to cut out things such as people, trees, and houses from construction paper. Then, glue them onto sheet of dark paper.

2 Use white crayon to draw falling snow. Pull apart the cotton ball; then, glue it onto the drawing for heavy snow.

3 Use black marker for shadows in the snow.

MORE ART FUN!

☆ Glue three cotton balls onto construction paper for a snowman.

☆ Use scissors to cut out things such as mittens, scarves, and hats from wrapping paper; then glue them onto figures in snow scene.

☆ Read *Snow!* by Roy McKie and P.D. Eastman.

☆ Have you ever made snow angels in the snow or sand angels in the sand at the beach? Lie down on your back in the snow or sand, and move your outstretched arms up and down beside you in the snow or sand. When you stand up, you'll see an angel print. How **cold** was it in the snow? How **hot** was it in the sand?

RECYCLED & FOUND ART

*If you've run out of art supplies,
here's what will save the day,
Take another look at the things
you might have thrown away!*

Paper Trees

*Save the paper in your house
to make something great,
Why throw it all away
when you can use it to create!*

HERE'S WHAT YOU NEED

Three sheets of used paper

Tape

Child safety scissors

Poster paint

Paintbrush

Paper Trees

*Save the paper in your house
to make something great,
Why throw it all away
when you can use it to create!*

HERE'S WHAT YOU NEED

Three sheets of used paper

Tape

Child safety scissors

Poster paint

Paintbrush

RECYCLED & FOUND ART

*If you've run out of art supplies,
here's what will save the day,
Take another look at the things
you might have thrown away!*

HERE'S WHAT YOU DO

1 Roll three sheets of paper lengthwise into a tube (do not wrap too tightly). Then, tape the tube together.

2 Use scissors to cut slits one inch (2.5 cm) apart and four inches (10 cm) deep, all the way around the tube.

3 Gently pull up on an inside fringe, until the branches of a tree appear.

4 Use poster paint to paint the tree.

ROLL 3 SHEETS OF PAPER TOGETHER INTO A TUBE

CUT SLITS AROUND THE TUBE

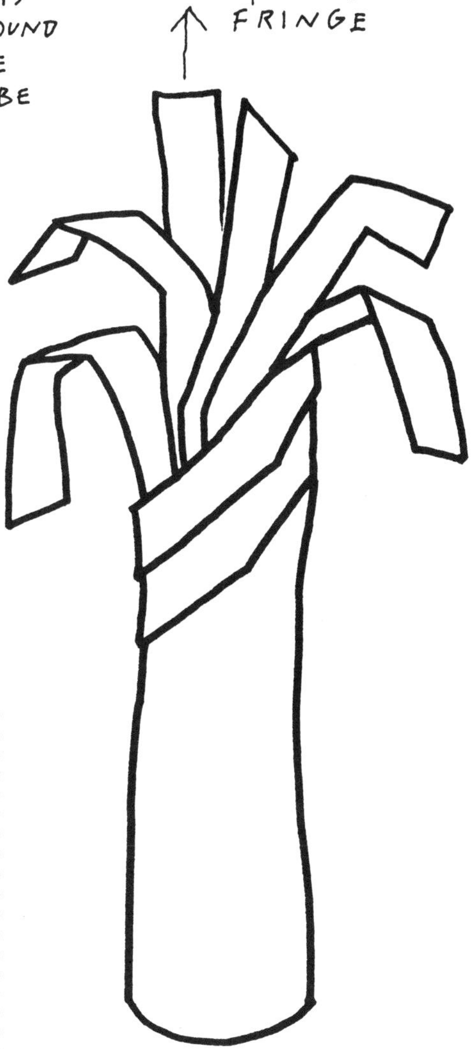

GENTLY PULL UP INSIDE FRINGE

MORE ART FUN!

☆ Use scissors to cut out fruits or flowers from construction paper, then glue them onto the tree.

☆ Read Shel Silverstein's *The Giving Tree*. Do you have a favorite tree? Take some lemonade or cocoa and go sit by it. Think about how your tree makes you feel.

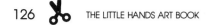

Cardboard Tube Puppets

You can make a funny puppet
who's tall and skinny, too,
Create it from a cardboard tube,
then say, "How do you do!"

HERE'S WHAT YOU NEED

Cardboard tube
from paper towel roll

Small brown paper bag

Newspaper

White craft glue

Scraps of construction paper

Tape

HERE'S WHAT YOU DO

1 Partially stuff brown paper bag with newspaper. Push the cardboard tube up into the opening of the bag; then tape around base of bag to secure it to the tube.

2 Use scissors to cut out puppet's eyes, nose, and mouth from construction paper. Glue them onto the bag.

3 Hold cardboard tube for a puppet show.

PARTIALLY STUFF BAG WITH NEWSPAPER

PUSH TUBE UP INTO BAG BOTTOM

TAPE BAG BOTTOM

CUT OUT EYES, NOSE, AND MOUTH

MORE ART FUN!

☆ Use scissors to cut puppet's arms out from shirt cardboard and glue them onto sides of cardboard tube. Cover tube in scrap fabric for puppet's costume. Glue on yarn scraps for puppet's hair.

☆ There are many ways to make a puppet show theater. All you need is a place to hide the puppeteer (that is you) while the puppets perform. How about sitting behind a sofa and having the puppets perform on the top of the sofa's back? What other instant puppet theaters can you create?

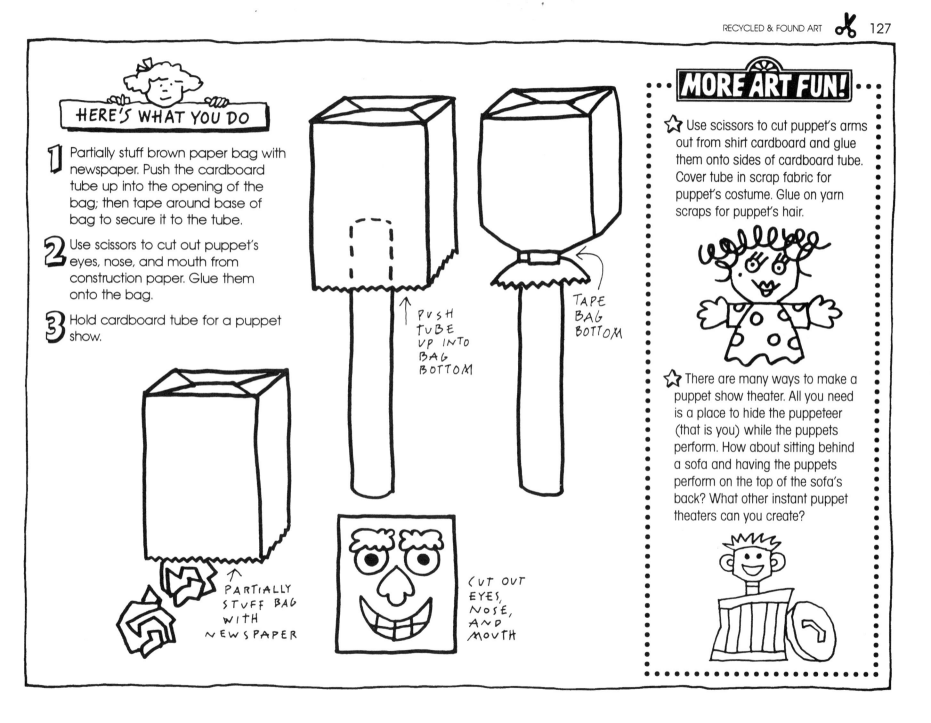

Cardboard Box Neighborhood

It's great to get a gift,
wrapped and nicely tied,
Have fun with the box,
and don't forget what's inside!

HERE'S WHAT YOU NEED

Cardboard boxes

Brown paper bags (cut open)

Masking tape

Child safety scissors

Markers

White craft glue

Scraps of construction paper

HERE'S WHAT YOU DO

1 Tightly wrap boxes in brown paper; then tape to hold in place.

2 Use scissors to cut out windows and doors from construction paper.

3 Glue on windows and doors; then stand the boxes upright for houses.

4 Use markers to draw things such as shutters, roof, and chimney on the houses. Make additional box houses for a neighborhood street.

MORE ART FUN!

☆ Use scissors to cut out things such as food, toys, and clothing from old magazines. Glue them in box's windows for stores.

☆ Ask a grown-up to help you locate a huge box from an appliance store. With grown-up help, cut out windows and doors. Now use all sorts of fabric and paper scraps to decorate your house. Then, move right inside!

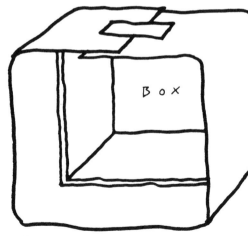

WRAP BOX IN BROWN PAPER

CUT OUT DOORS AND WINDOWS

GLUE ON DOORS AND WINDOWS

Papier-Mache Bowls

Newspapers get out of date,
they're old the very next day,
Cut the pages into strips
and use for papier-mache!

HERE'S WHAT YOU NEED

Newspaper

Paper towels

Papier-mache paste
(see recipe on page 147)

Small bowl

Aluminum pie pan

Liquid vegetable oil

Child safety scissors

HERE'S WHAT YOU DO

1 Cover table with newspaper.

2 Use scissors to cut sheets of newspaper into one-inch (2.5 cm) by five-inch (12.5 cm) strips.

3 Lightly grease bottom of bowl with vegetable oil.

4 Pour papier-mache paste into pie tin. Dip one strip at a time into paste. Run the strip between a thumb and forefinger to remove excess paste.

5 Wrap two or three layers of strips over bowl. Smooth out lumps and bumps and trim the edges.

6 After 24 hours drying time, add two or three additional layers. As a final layer, dip strips of paper toweling into the paste and cover over all.

7 Allow papier-mache to dry completely, then slip it off the bowl.

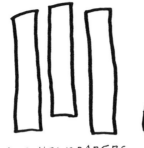

CUT NEWSPAPERS INTO 1"×5" STRIPS

LIGHTLY GREASE BOWL BOTTOM

DIP STRIPS IN PAPIER-MACHE PASTE

WRAP TWO OR THREE LAYERS OF STRIPS OVER BOWL

LET DRY FOR 24 HOURS. THEN ADD MORE LAYERS

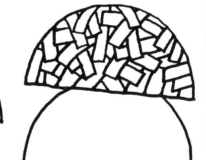

WHEN DRY, SLIP PAPIER-MACHE BOWL OFF FORM

MORE ART FUN!

☆ Paint the dried bowl with poster paints.

☆ Do a final layer with bits of brightly colored tissue paper.

☆ Set up a box in your house to collect newspapers for recycling. Visit your local recycling center to see what they do with the paper. Ask lots of questions.

NEWSPAPERS

Woven Berry Baskets

*When you're done eating berries,
save the basket they came in,
Make it something beautiful,
weaving yarn through with a pin!*

HERE'S WHAT YOU NEED

Plastic berry basket

Safety pin

**Strands of thin ribbon
6 inches (15 cm) long**

Child safety scissors

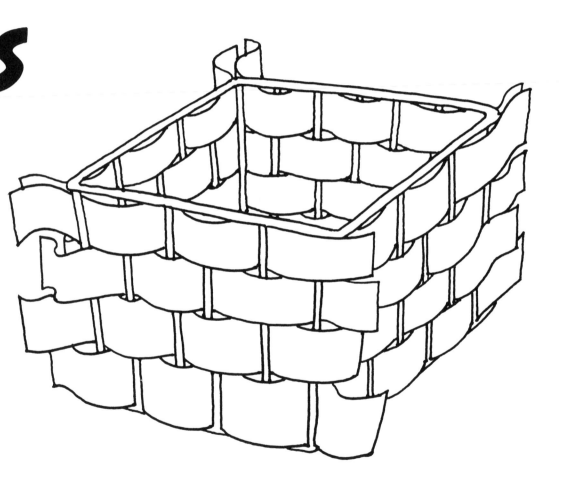

HERE'S WHAT YOU DO

1 Use scissors to cut ribbon into six-inch (15 cm) pieces.

2 Attach safety pin to the end of one piece of ribbon. Use the pin as a needle to weave in and out of the plastic mesh (to keep ribbon in place, do not pull it all the way through the mesh).

3 Attach the pin to each piece of ribbon and continue weaving until basket is covered with ribbons.

MORE ART FUN!

☆ Weave natural materials such as reeds, long grasses, dandelions, and jute through the basket.

☆ In early spring, pick some violets or other early flowers (ask permission first) and fill your basket. Ring the doorbell of a friendly neighbor and leave your basket at the door for a springtime surprise.

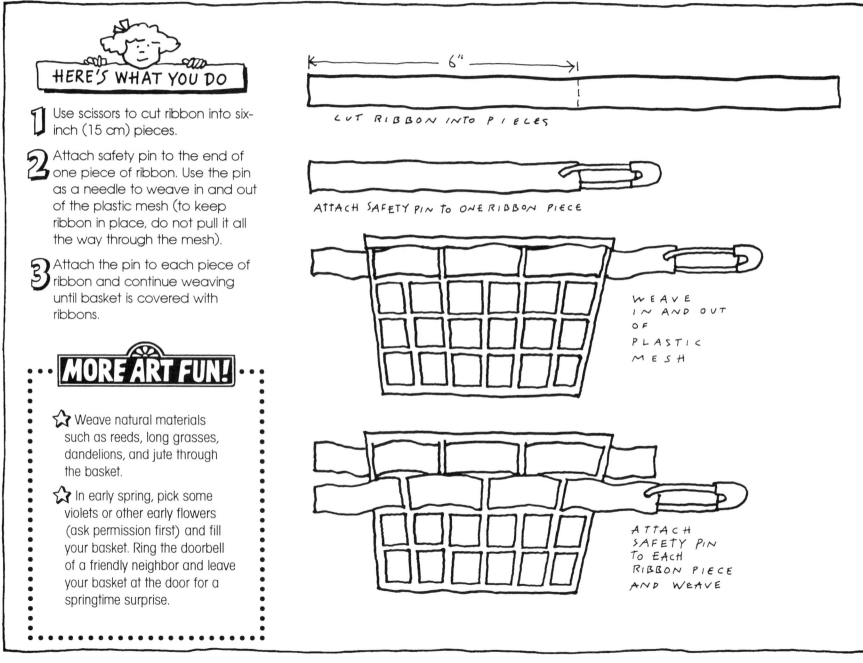

6"

CUT RIBBON INTO PIECES

ATTACH SAFETY PIN TO ONE RIBBON PIECE

WEAVE IN AND OUT OF PLASTIC MESH

ATTACH SAFETY PIN TO EACH RIBBON PIECE AND WEAVE

Treasure Box

*Glue pasta on a box,
then when it is dried,
Close the lid and keep
treasures hidden inside!*

HERE'S WHAT YOU DO

1 Cover table with newspaper. Pour glue into pie pan and add a few drops of water.

2 Use brush to spread a thick layer of glue onto lid of box (work on one small section at a time).

3 Glue pasta close together onto box until lid is covered; then allow to dry completely.

4 Paint the box with poster paint.

MORE ART FUN!

⭐ Crumple small pieces of colored tissue paper into balls. Glue tissue paper balls onto lid of box until completely covered.

⭐ Arrange pasta in your initials and glue to box. Then using another pasta shape, make a border around the top of box.

⭐ Instead of pasta, use other found art objects such as pebbles, sea glass, buttons, acorns, or whatever you can collect in or around your house.

HERE'S WHAT YOU NEED

Small cardboard box (with lid)

Small pasta shapes
(shells, wheels, or macaroni)

White craft glue

Poster paint

Paintbrushes (2)

Aluminum pie pan

Newspaper

Odds & Ends Picture

*Scraps are bits and pieces
we pay no attention to,
Gather them together,
and create something brand new!*

HERE'S WHAT YOU NEED

Cardboard

White craft glue

Scrap materials

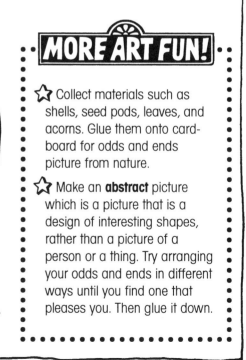

HERE'S WHAT YOU DO

1. Arrange scrap materials such as fabric, wallpaper, yarn, greeting cards, wrapping paper, and sandpaper onto cardboard (move them around to achieve desired placement).

2. Glue materials onto cardboard; then allow to dry completely for odds and ends picture.

MORE ART FUN!

☆ Collect materials such as shells, seed pods, leaves, and acorns. Glue them onto cardboard for odds and ends picture from nature.

☆ Make an **abstract** picture which is a picture that is a design of interesting shapes, rather than a picture of a person or a thing. Try arranging your odds and ends in different ways until you find one that pleases you. Then glue it down.

Paper Bag Vests

Don't throw away those grocery bags,
when the shopping's done,
Turn them into paper vests,
try making more than one!

HERE'S WHAT YOU NEED

Brown paper grocery bag

Child safety scissors

Ribbon

Stapler

Poster paint

Paintbrush

HERE'S WHAT YOU DO

1. Lay grocery bag flat with opening at the bottom. Use scissors to cut up the center of the bag.

2. Cut a round opening into top of bag for neck. Cut out round arm holes in each side of the bag.

3. Cut ribbon in half, each piece should be about 6 inches (15 cm) long. Staple ribbons to vest to tie closed.

4. Paint vest with poster paint. Allow to dry completely.

MORE ART FUN!

☆ Use scissors to cut fringes on the vest.

☆ Cut sponges into shapes, dip into poster paint, and print onto vest. Allow to dry completely. Glue fabric scraps and trim onto vest.

☆ Glue iridescent strips to front and back of vest and wear with your helmet when riding your bike.

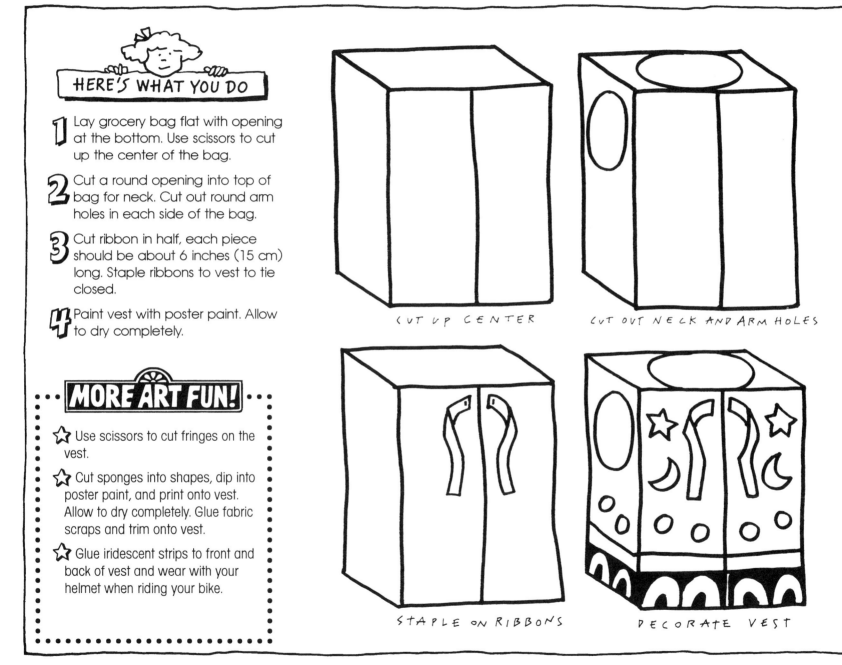

CUT UP CENTER

CUT OUT NECK AND ARM HOLES

STAPLE ON RIBBONS

DECORATE VEST

Oatmeal Carton Drum

*When your oatmeal's finished,
down to the last crumb,
Use your imagination
to make a special drum!*

HERE'S WHAT YOU NEED

Oatmeal or cornmeal box

Construction paper

Markers

Tape

Child safety scissors

White craft glue

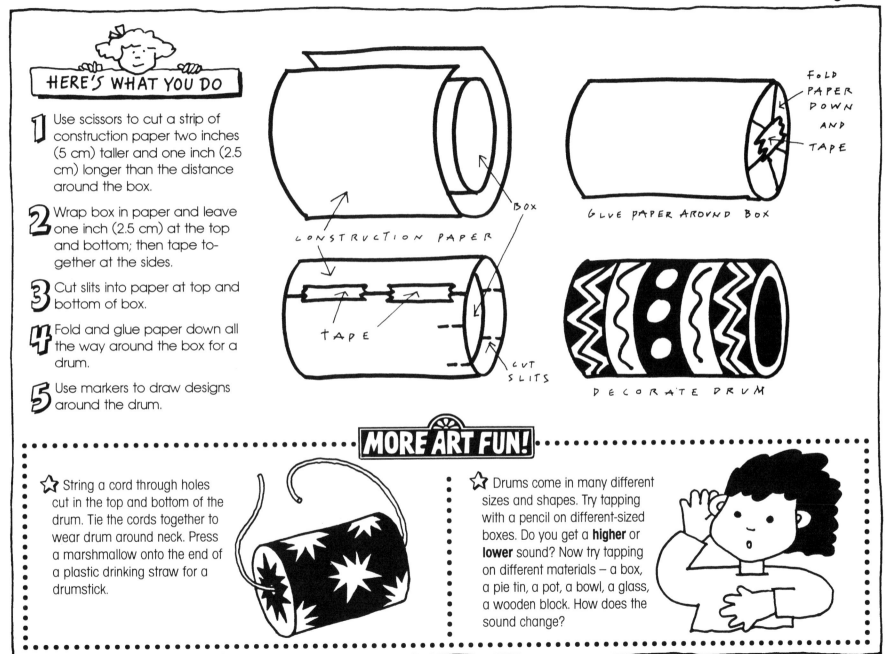

HERE'S WHAT YOU DO

1 Use scissors to cut a strip of construction paper two inches (5 cm) taller and one inch (2.5 cm) longer than the distance around the box.

2 Wrap box in paper and leave one inch (2.5 cm) at the top and bottom; then tape together at the sides.

3 Cut slits into paper at top and bottom of box.

4 Fold and glue paper down all the way around the box for a drum.

5 Use markers to draw designs around the drum.

CONSTRUCTION PAPER

BOX

GLUE PAPER AROUND BOX

FOLD PAPER DOWN AND TAPE

TAPE

CUT SLITS

DECORATE DRUM

MORE ART FUN!

☆ String a cord through holes cut in the top and bottom of the drum. Tie the cords together to wear drum around neck. Press a marshmallow onto the end of a plastic drinking straw for a drumstick.

☆ Drums come in many different sizes and shapes. Try tapping with a pencil on different-sized boxes. Do you get a **higher** or **lower** sound? Now try tapping on different materials — a box, a pie tin, a pot, a bowl, a glass, a wooden block. How does the sound change?

Dragon Sock Puppet

Socks come in pairs,
but if you're missing one,
Make a sock puppet,
and you'll have lots of fun!

HERE'S WHAT YOU NEED

An old sock

Red felt

Scrap fabric

Child safety scissors

White craft glue

HERE'S WHAT YOU DO

1. Use scissors to cut out an oval shape from red felt. Cut out eyes and ears from fabric scraps.

2. Place a hand in the sock with four fingers on top and a thumb on the bottom. Use the other hand to press in between fingers and thumb to form a mouth.

3. Glue the red felt into the mouth; then glue on the puppet's eyes and ears, and any other dragon features you would like your puppet to have.

RED FELT

OVAL (FOR MOUTH)

FABRIC SCRAP

EARS (CUT 2)

EYES (CUT 2)

HAND

SOCK

GLUE EYES, EARS, AND MOUTH ON SOCK

MORE ART FUN!

⭐ Glue on fabric trim and yarn for the puppet's eyebrows and hair.

⭐ Turn a table or large cardboard box into a stage for a puppet show.

PUPPET SHOW

⭐ Read *Socks for Supper* by Jack Kent.

⭐ Listen to the song "Puff the Magic Dragon" by Peter, Paul, and Mary.

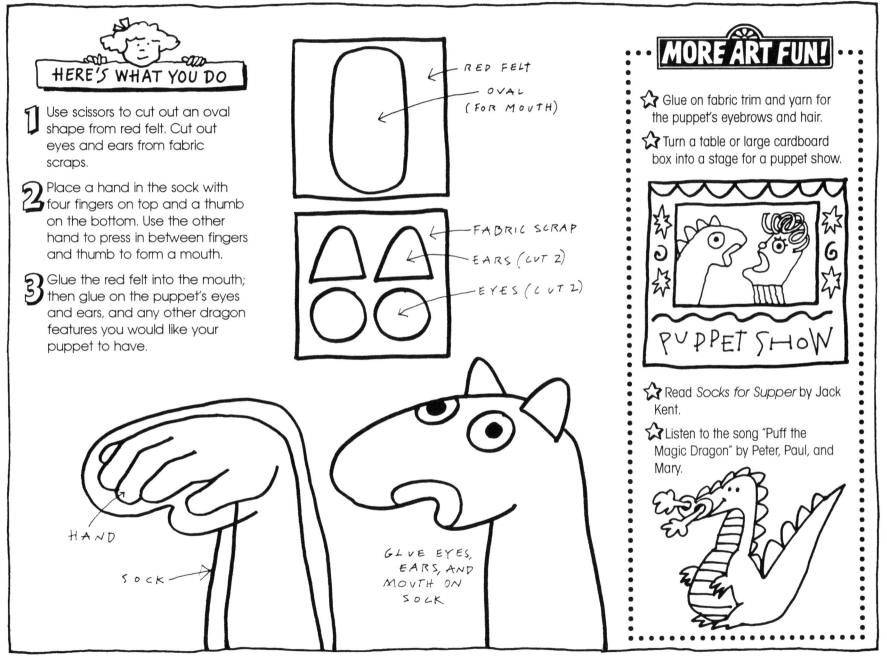

Recycle Sculpture

*Take packing from a box
— avoid a landfill site —
Use it for a sculpture,
try building one tonight!*

HERE'S WHAT YOU NEED

Styrofoam blocks, packing popcorn, packing noodles

*Dull knife

Toothpicks

HERE'S WHAT YOU DO

1 Use the dull knife to cut styrofoam blocks into a variety of shapes and sizes. Save a flat piece for sculpture's base.

2 Use toothpicks to attach the blocks and other found materials to each other for a sculpture; then press into styrofoam base.

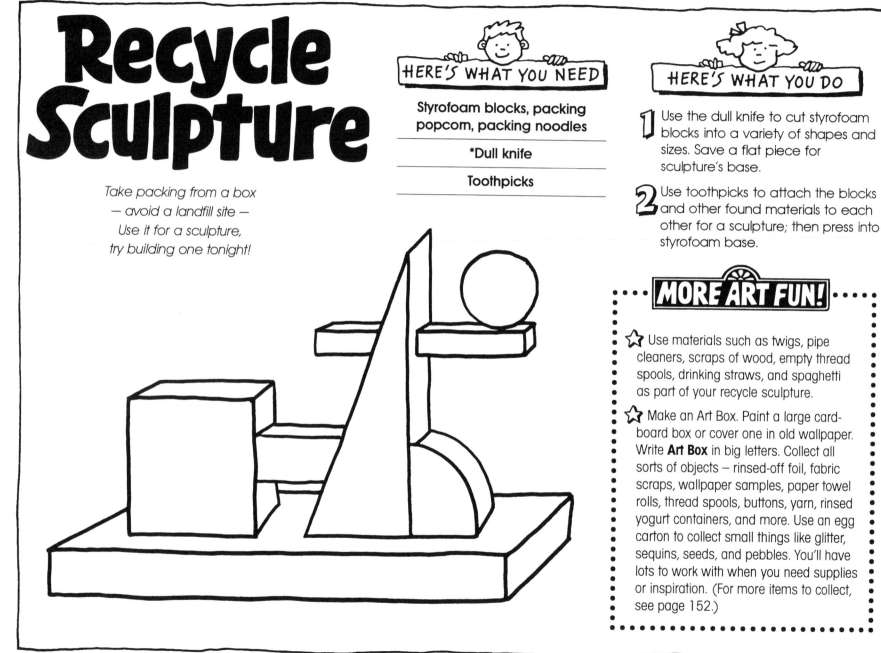

MORE ART FUN!

☆ Use materials such as twigs, pipe cleaners, scraps of wood, empty thread spools, drinking straws, and spaghetti as part of your recycle sculpture.

☆ Make an Art Box. Paint a large cardboard box or cover one in old wallpaper. Write **Art Box** in big letters. Collect all sorts of objects — rinsed-off foil, fabric scraps, wallpaper samples, paper towel rolls, thread spools, buttons, yarn, rinsed yogurt containers, and more. Use an egg carton to collect small things like glitter, sequins, seeds, and pebbles. You'll have lots to work with when you need supplies or inspiration. (For more items to collect, see page 152.)

Wire Sculpture

When you bend a piece of wire,
it will always stay,
Unless you change your mind,
and bend the other way!

HERE'S WHAT YOU NEED

Florist's wire or other bendable wire scraps

Play dough (see recipe on page 148)

Child safety scissors

HERE'S WHAT YOU DO

1. Use scissors to cut wire into 18-inch (45 cm) pieces.

2. Flatten a ball of play dough for base of sculpture.

3. Bend the wire into different shapes; then press ends into play dough for a sculpture.

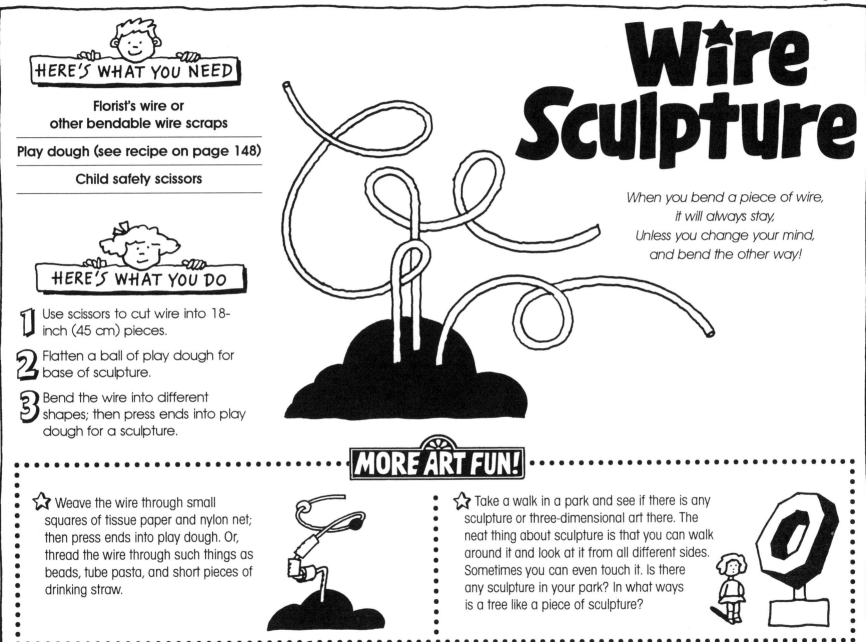

MORE ART FUN!

☆ Weave the wire through small squares of tissue paper and nylon net; then press ends into play dough. Or, thread the wire through such things as beads, tube pasta, and short pieces of drinking straw.

☆ Take a walk in a park and see if there is any sculpture or three-dimensional art there. The neat thing about sculpture is that you can walk around it and look at it from all different sides. Sometimes you can even touch it. Is there any sculpture in your park? In what ways is a tree like a piece of sculpture?

Autumn Wreath

When the first chill is in the air,
And summer's colors fade.
Collect some of nature's gifts,
A pretty wreath to be made.

HERE'S WHAT YOU NEED

Piece of cardboard

*Sharp knife

White craft glue

Pinecones, leaves, acorns,
hickory nuts, seed pods

Long reeds or
pieces of scrap yarn

HERE'S WHAT YOU DO

1 Ask a grown-up to cut a large circle from cardboard. Then, cut inner circle so you are left with a wreath shape.

2 Glue pinecones, leaves, acorns, hickory nuts, and seed pods to wreath shape until cardboard is completely covered.

3 Make a bow with some long reeds or pieces of scrap yarn.

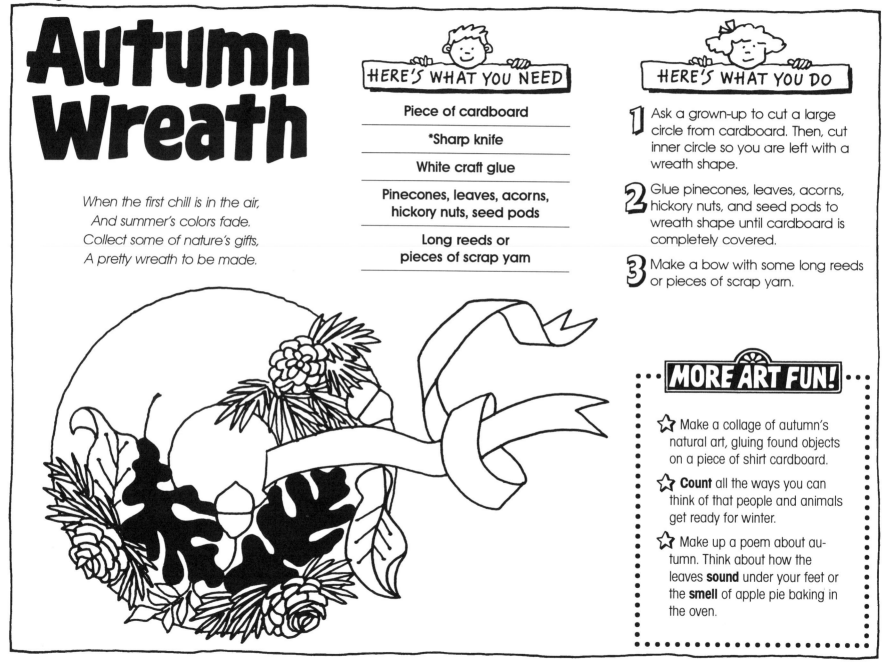

MORE ART FUN!

☆ Make a collage of autumn's natural art, gluing found objects on a piece of shirt cardboard.

☆ **Count** all the ways you can think of that people and animals get ready for winter.

☆ Make up a poem about autumn. Think about how the leaves **sound** under your feet or the **smell** of apple pie baking in the oven.

APPENDIX

Appendix

Recipes for Homemade Art Supplies

Flour Paste

HERE'S WHAT YOU NEED

½ cup (125 ml) flour

⅔ cup (150 ml) water

Oil of peppermint or oil of wintergreen

HERE'S WHAT YOU DO

1 Mix the flour and water together. Stir until paste has a creamy consistency.

2 Add a few drops of the oil, as a preservative. This will make about ½ pint (250 ml).

Cornstarch Paste

HERE'S WHAT YOU NEED

3/4 cup (175 ml) water

2 tablespoons (25 ml) light Karo syrup

1 teaspoon (5 ml) white vinegar

1/2 cup (67 ml) cornstarch

3/4 cup (175 ml) water

Oil of wintergreen

HERE'S WHAT YOU DO

1 Mix 3/4 cup (175 ml) water, Karo syrup, and vinegar together in a saucepan. Ask a grown-up to help you bring the mixture to a full boil.

2 Mix the cornstarch with the second 3/4 cup (175 ml) of water, and add slowly to the boiling mixture. Stir constantly to avoid lumps.

3 Let the mixture stand overnight before use. If a few drops of the oil are added as a preservative, this paste will be good for about two months. This will make 1 pint (500 ml) of paste.

Papier-Mache Paste

Use this paste with strips of paper to cover a form. Let each layer dry before adding another layer.

HERE'S WHAT YOU NEED

3 cups (750 ml) cold water

1 1/2 cups (375 ml) flour

Oil of peppermint

HERE'S WHAT YOU DO

1 In a heavy saucepan, stir flour into cold water. Ask a grown-up to cook over low heat until the mixture thickens to a creamy paste.

2 Cool; then add a few drops of peppermint oil.

Self-Hardening Salt Clay

HERE'S WHAT YOU NEED

1½ cups (375 ml) salt

4 cups (1 l) flour

1½ cups (375 ml) water

1 teaspoon (5 ml) alum
(as preservative if clay is not baked)

HERE'S WHAT YOU DO

1. Mix the dry ingredients together in a plastic bowl; then add water gradually.

2. When dough forms a ball around the spoon, knead the dough well, adding water if it is too crumbly.

3. This clay can also be baked. Set the oven to 300° F (150° C) and bake small shapes for 30-40 minutes or until hard.

Play Dough Clay

(NON-HARDENING)

HERE'S WHAT YOU NEED

2 cups (500 ml) flour

1 cup (250 ml) salt

1 teaspoon (5 ml) cream of tartar

2 tablespoons (25 ml) oil

1 teaspoon (5 ml) food coloring

2 cups (500 ml) water

HERE'S WHAT YOU DO

1. Mix ingredients in a saucepan. Ask a grown-up for help in cooking over medium heat, stirring constantly, until dough leaves sides of pan.

2. Remove from pan, and when cool to the touch, knead for a few minutes.

Cloud Dough

This dough is oily, but it is extremely pliable and easy for very young children to use.

HERE'S WHAT YOU NEED

1/2 cup (125 ml) water (or more)

1/2 cup (125 ml) cooking oil

2 cups (500 ml) flour

2 cups (500 ml) salt

Food coloring

Peppermint oil

HERE'S WHAT YOU DO

1 Mix together the cooking oil, flour, and salt. Add a few drops of the food color to the water.

2 Gradually add the water (additional water may be needed to bind the dough). Add a few drops of the peppermint oil.

3 Knead the mixture until smooth and pliable.

Cornstarch Dough

HERE'S WHAT YOU NEED

1/2 cup (125 ml) water

1 cup (250 ml) baking soda

1/2 cup (125 ml) cornstarch

HERE'S WHAT YOU DO

1 Mix together the soda, water, and cornstarch in a heavy saucepan. Ask a grown-up to cook over low heat, stirring with a wooden spoon until the mixture becomes thick.

2 Add a few drops of food coloring. Cool and knead until it's smooth. Use dough for modeling or roll out and cut shapes.

3 Air-dry dough before painting. Store dough in a plastic bag in the refrigerator.

Sawdust Dough

This dough has an interesting texture for small sculpture projects.

HERE'S WHAT YOU NEED

2 cups (500 ml) sawdust

1 cup (250 ml) wallpaper paste

Water

HERE'S WHAT YOU DO

1 Mix the dry paste with the sawdust. Slowly add water until a thick dough forms.

2 Model into shapes. Let harden overnight.

Finger Paint

Add a sprinkling of powdered soap flakes (not liquid) to either of these recipes to help paint glide over the paper and to make clean-up easier.

HERE'S WHAT YOU DO

Mix 2 parts of liquid laundry starch with 1 part powdered tempera paint or a few drops of food color as you paint on the paper.

or

Mix flour and cold water into a paste. Add food coloring or powdered tempera paint on the paper as you paint.

Soap Paint

This paint dries with a three-dimensional effect. Colored sand or glitter will adhere to the paint without using glue. Work with the paint on heavy paper or cardboard. Dispose of paint in a trash can, as it will clog a sink drain.

HERE'S WHAT YOU NEED

1 cup (250 ml) soap flakes (do not use soap powder)

½ cup (125 ml) cold water

Food coloring or powdered tempera paint

HERE'S WHAT YOU DO

1 Put cold water into a bowl, add soap flakes, and beat with a mixer until stiff (the consistency of beaten egg whites).

2 Add food color or powdered paint; beat thoroughly.

Squeeze Bottle Paint

HERE'S WHAT YOU NEED

Flour

Salt

Poster paint

Plastic squeeze bottles

HERE'S WHAT YOU DO

1 Mix equal parts of flour and salt. Add paint to form a paste.

2 Pour into plastic squeeze bottles. Squeeze paint onto heavy paper or cardboard.

Appendix

B

Recycled & Found Art Materials

Help children collect, sort, and store these wonderful found art supplies. Use egg cartons, jewelry gift boxes, margarine tubs, and yogurt containers for storage. These treasures are an inspiration to the creative spirit as well as a good lesson in recycling and resource conservation.

Aluminum foil (washed and dried)
Bendable wire scraps
Buttons
Cellophane "windows" on pasta packaging
Cardboard boxes
Cardboard scraps
Cardboard tubes
Cereal boxes
Clothespins
Combs
Cotton balls
Crepe paper streamers (used)
Dried beans and peas
Dried flowers and grasses
Driftwood
Egg cartons
Eggshells (washed)
Fabric trim
Feathers
Felt scraps
Florist's wire
Gift wrap paper (used)
Greeting cards
Magazines and catalogs
Manufacturer's scraps
Margarine tubs
Milk cartons

Newspaper
Nylon net
Old barrettes
Old jewelry (especially pin and earring backings)
Packing popcorn
Paper bags
Pasta (uncooked)
Pebbles and stones
Pie tins
Plastic lids
Popsicle sticks
Ribbons
Sawdust
Scrap fabric
Sea glass
Seashells
Socks
Sponges
Stirrer sticks
Straws
Styrofoam trays (from fruits or vegetables only)
Toothpicks
Wallpaper (scraps and sample books)
Wooden beads
Wood dowels
Wood scraps
Yogurt containers

Index

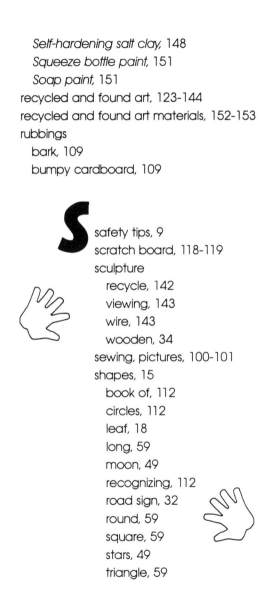

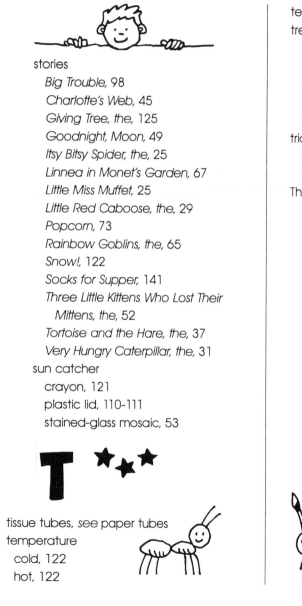

More *Kids Can!* Books from

Williamson Publishing

To order additional copies of **The Little Hands Art Book**, please enclose $12.95 per copy plus $2.50 for shipping. Follow "To Order" instructions on the last page. Thank you.

ECOART!
Earth-Friendly Art & Craft Experiences for 3- to 9-year-olds
by Laurie Carlson

What better way to learn to love and care for the Earth than through creative art play! Laurie Carlson's latest book is packed with 150 projects using only recyclable, reusable, or nature's own found art materials. These fabulous activities are sure to please any child!

160 pages, 11 x 8 1/2, 400 illustrations
Quality paperback, $12.95

THE KIDS' MULTICULTURAL ART BOOK
Art & Craft Experiences from Around the World
by Alexandra M. Terzian

Alexandra Terzian brings an unsurpassed enthusiasm to the hands-on multicultural art experience. Children will reach across continents and oceans with paper, paste, and paints, while absorbing basic sensibilities about the wondrous cultures of others. Children will learn by making such things as the *Korhogo Mud Cloth* and the *Wodaabe Mirror Pouch* from Africa, the *Chippewa Dream Catcher* of the American Indian, the *Kokeshi Doll* of Japan, *Chinese Egg Painting*, the Mexican *Folk Art Tree of Life*, the *Twirling Palm Puppet* from India, and the Guatemalan *Green Toad Bank*. A virtual feast of multicultural art and craft experiences!

160 pages, 11 x 8 1/2, over 400 how-to-do-it illustrations
Quality paperback, $12.95

KIDS COOK!
Fabulous Food For The Whole Family
by Sarah Williamson and Zachary Williamson

Here's a cookbook written for kids by two teenagers who know what kids like to eat! *Kids Cook!* is filled with over 150 recipes for great-tasting foods that kids ages 8 and up can cook for themselves and for their families and friends, too. Try breakfast bonanzas like *Breakfast Sundaes*, great lunches including *Chicken Shirt Pocket*, super salads like *A Whale of a Fruit Salad*, quick snacks and easy extras like *Nacho Nibbles*, delicious dinners including *Pizza Originale*, and dynamite desserts and soda fountain treats including *Chocolate Surprise Cupcakes*. All recipes are for "real," healthy foods — not cutesy recipes that are no fun to eat. Plus Nutri Notes, Safety First, and plenty of special menus for Father's Day, Grandma's Teatime, picnics, and parties. One terrific book!

160 pages, 11 x 8 1/2, Over 150 recipes, illustrations
Quality paperback, $12.95

THE KIDS' SCIENCE BOOK
Creative Experiences for Hands-On Fun
by Robert Hirschfeld and Nancy White

Science has never been so accessible to the hearts and minds of kids before! Learning and hands-on fun are one and the same as kids explore the human body and make a model lung, use levers to make a jumping coin game, discover the world of spiders while making an amazing climbing spider, plus learn about plants, dinosaurs, color, the five senses, planet earth, magnets, and water and air pressure. *The Kids' Science Book* is crammed with ideas that pique kids' curiosity and with creative activities to solidify the learning experience.

160 pages, 11 x 8$\frac{1}{2}$, 100 activities, over 150 illustrations
Quality paperback, $12.95

Winner of the Benjamin Franklin Award!

KIDS MAKE MUSIC!
Clapping and Tapping from Bach to Rock
by Avery Hart and Paul Mantell

No instruments necessary — just hands, feet, and wiggly bodies! Kids are natural music makers, and with the kid-loving music makers, Avery Hart and Paul Mantell, children everywhere will be doing the *Dinosaur Dance*, singing the *Dishwashin' Blues*, cleaning their rooms to *Rap*, belting it out in a *Jug Band* or *An Accidental Orchestra*, putting on a *Fairy Tale Opera*, learning to *Tap Dance* or creating a *Bona Fide Ballet* (homemade tutu included)! Those hands will be clapping, those feet will be tapping, those faces will be grinning, and they may be humming anything from Bach to Rock.

160 pages, 11 x 8$\frac{1}{2}$, with hundreds of illustrations
Quality paperback, $12.95

TALES ALIVE!
Ten Multicultural Folk Tales with Activities
by Susan Milord

Award-winning author, Susan Milord brings ten folk tales from around the world to life with a myriad of exciting, relevant hands-on activities. *Tales Alive!* will lock these universal stories into the hearts and minds of children for many years to follow. Includes wondrous stories from Australia, Argentina, China, Ghana, Canada, Russia, and other countries. A virtual feast of multicultural fun and learning!

128 pages, 8$\frac{1}{2}$ x 11, full-color illustrations
Quality paperback, $15.95

THE KIDS' WILDLIFE BOOK
Exploring Animal Worlds through Indoor/Outdoor Crafts & Experiences
by Warner Shedd

Mention bats to most kids and they will immediately tell you that bats are blind. Don't pick up that toad because it will give you warts — right? What most kids know about wildlife is stranger than, well, the fiction that it is! With awesome tales, facts and amusing anecdotes to make activities meaningful and fun, Warner Shedd's thoughtful approach fills children with wonder and respect for the creatures with whom they share this planet.

160 pages, 11 x 8$\frac{1}{2}$, with hundreds of illustrations, range maps, index
Quality paperback, $12.95

KIDS' CRAZY CONCOCTIONS
Mysterious Mixtures for Art & Craft Fun
by Jill Frankel Hauser

Mix it, stretch it, knead it, squish, squash, mush, and mash — however it's done, kids are bound to have endless hours of fun and learning as they concoct the craziest things. Hauser captures the imagination of kids with creative play filled with tangible results. Concoct your own watercolor cakes, almost-oil soap paint, temperas, crazy doughs. Make soap-on-a-rope, lick-it-later custom stickers, mega-monster face paints, stunning crepe paper bowls. Learn the whys, hows, and wherefores — and then, let the art start!

160 pages, 11 x 8½, over 300 illustrations
Quality paperback, $12.95

HANDS AROUND THE WORLD
365 Creative Ways to Build Cultural Awareness & Global Respect
by Susan Milord

Award-winning author Susan Milord invites children to experience, taste, and embrace the daily lives of children from the far corners of the earth. In 365 days of experiences, it tears down stereotypes and replaces them with the fascinating realities of our differences and our similarities. Children everywhere can plant and grow, write and tell stories, draw and craft, cook and eat, sing and dance, look and explore, as they learn to live in an atmosphere of global respect and cultural awareness that is born of personal experience.

160 pages, 11 x 8½, over 400 illustrations
Quality paperback, $12.95

Winner of the Parents' Choice Gold Award!

Over 200,000 copies sold!

THE KIDS' NATURE BOOK
365 Indoor/Outdoor Activities and Experiences
by Susan Milord

The Kids' Nature Book is loved by children, grandparents, and friends alike. Simple projects and activities emphasize fun while quietly reinforcing the wonder of the world we all share. Packed with facts and fun!

160 pages, 11 x 8½, 425 illustrations
Quality paperback, $12.95

Over 250,000 copies sold!

KIDS CREATE!
Art & Craft Experiences for 3- to 9-year-olds
by Laurie Carlson

What's the most important experience for children ages 3 to 9? Why, to create something by themselves. Carlson provides over 150 creative experiences ranging from making dinosaur sculptures to clay cactus gardens, from butterfly puppets to windsocks. Plenty of help for the parents working with the kids, too! A delightfully innovative book.

160 pages, 11 x 8½, over 400 illustrations
Quality paperback, $12.95

KIDS LEARN AMERICA!
Bringing Geography to Life with People, Places, & History
by Patricia Gordon and Reed C. Snow

Designed to help increase "geo-literacy," *Kids Learn America!* is not about memorizing. This creative and exciting new book is about making every region of our country come alive from within, about being connected to the earth and the people across this great expanse called America.•Activities and games targeted to the 50 states plus D.C. and Puerto Rico •The environment and natural resources •Geographic comparisons •Fascinating facts, famous people and places of each region. Let us all join together — kids, parents, friends, teachers, grandparents — and put America, its geography, its history, and its heritage back on the map!

176 pages, 11 x 8½, maps, illustrations
Quality paperback, $12.95

ADVENTURES IN ART
Art & Craft Experiences for 7- to 14-year-olds
by Susan Milord

Imagine an art book that encourages children to explore, to experience, to touch and to see, to learn and to create...imagine a true adventure in art. Here's a book that teaches artisans' skills without stifling creativity. Covers making handmade papers, puppets, masks, paper seascapes, seed art, tin can lantern, berry ink, still life, silk screen, batiking, carving, and so much more. Perfect for the older child. Let the adventure begin!

160 pages, 11 x 8½, 500 illustrations
Quality paperback, $12.95

KIDS AND WEEKENDS!
Creative Ways to Make Special Days
by Avery Hart and Paul Mantell

Packed with truly creative ways to play, have fun, learn, grow, and build self-esteem and positive relationships, this book is a must for every parent, grandparent, babysitter and teacher. Hart and Mantell will inspire us all to transform some part of every weekend — even if it is only 30 minutes — into a special experience. Everything from back-yard nature to putting on a magic show to creating a bird sanctuary to writing a book about yourself to environmentally-sound activities indoors and out. Whatever your interests, no matter how busy you are, kids and their families will savor special weekend moments.

176 pages, 11 x 8½, over 400 illustrations
Quality paperback, $12.95